Series

Quality Management in Services

 ST⌐ ⌐D LOAN

Managing Service Quality
(Volume II)

Edited by:

Paul Kunst
Jos Lemmink

P·C·P
Paul Chapman
Publishing Ltd

Paul Chapman Publishing Ltd
144 Liverpool Road
London
N1 1LA

British Library Cataloguing in Publication Data

Managing Service Quality. – Vol.2. –
    (Quality Management in Services Series)
    I. Kunst, Paul   II. Lemmink, Jos
    III. Series
    658.562

ISBN 1–85396–330–5

Printed and bound by Athenaeum Press, Gateshead.

A B C D E F G H   9 8 7 6

Preface

When we first started this series on Quality Management in Services, we stated that business quality would be seen as one of the major competitive factors in the next decade. The situation has not changed much since then. The management of quality in organisations is a topic that continues to receive ever-increasing attention and yet not all the answers have been found. Answers are lacking both from a practical point of view and from a more theoretical perspective. Another remark we made a few years ago is also relevant: solutions evolve from interdisciplinary approaches. Once again, this holds true for both theory and practice.

Has there been no progress, then, over the past few years? The answer is yes, advances have been made. Nevertheless, the problem is that the environment is still changing. Important developments that have taken place affect service to customers, for example, the increased innovation in the telecommunications sector and the increased need for companies to improve service quality in highly competitive environments. Another development in services is the need to acquire ISO certification. All these developments have an impact on the structuring, functioning and organisation of the whole service delivery process.

What do we see as our role? By publishing innovative, new, challenging or even controversial research, we hope to contribute to the overall development of business quality. To be more precise, we feel that in order to define a research framework for service quality, it is important to state a number of research fundamentals. The research can focus on the organisation or the individual. At the same time, researchers can use established methods as well as emerging methods. At this moment in time, most researchers use established methods, including statistical techniques, systems analysis, quality management techniques and survey instruments. In order to advance service quality research, researchers should use other, perhaps neglected, techniques such as individually focused research and emerging methods such as fuzzy decision making and applied chaos theory. Most research at present is empirical and technique-driven. There is a definite need for more theory-driven research. We need more and better models: for example, the service quality model (SERVQUAL) needs more theoretical underpinning. Rather than the overwhelming number of empirical studies and comments that are being published, new or alternative models must be developed in the near future.

By stimulating this research, the workshops organised by the EIASM (European Institute on Advanced Studies in Management) have been and are very fruitful. When in a few years' time, we look back at our efforts, we will find out whether we have been on the right track.

In 1991, the first workshop on Quality Management in Services was organised in Brussels. Its objective was to bring together a group of experts from different disciplines to study the field of the management of service quality, and at the same time close the gap between research and practice. As we mentioned previously, another observation was that there is a lack of multi-disciplinary studies and theory. Therefore, the second objective was to encourage the different disciplines to exchange ideas, theories and approaches in order to get joint research started.

In 1992, 1993, 1994 and 1995, further Quality Management in Services workshops were organised in Maastricht, Helsinki, Paris and Tilburg, respectively. In two subsequent books* containing mainly papers from these workshops, we tried to register the research and progress in the field. With the present book, a total of 32 articles have been published. We are now able to make two observations.

First, the series includes contributions from all over Europe, and some from the United States and Canada. There is no doubt a broad interest in the topic exists. Second, the contributions are in the areas of marketing, operations, organisation, and human resource management. In other words, different disciplines feel the need to contribute to the topic. However, from Table 1 one might conclude that there is a gradual shift in emphasis to chapters on marketing.

Table 1   Topics from different disciplines over time

discipline	first book	second book	third book
marketing	4	8	6
other	8	4	2
TOTAL	12	12	8

We hope that in future workshops, we will receive more input from other disciplines and that some of these will be truly multi-disciplinary. By the time this book has been published, we will know what 'Tilburg, The Netherlands, 1995' has produced. In 1996, the Service Quality Management Workshop will be co-organised in Madrid together with the Service Productivity Workshop of EIASM.

This volume contains papers from the 1994 workshop in Marne-la-Vallée (Paris). As before, we feel that interesting papers have emerged from this workshop. After the careful, and sometimes difficult, editing process, this resulted in the following contributions.

Chapter 1, by Andrea Bonaccorsi and Anna Fiorentino, deals with an application of transaction cost theory to intra-company service exchanges as compared to market exchanges. The authors concluded that markets and hierarchies in service situations tend to differ in qualitative terms in the way they coordinate economic transactions.

Chapter 2, by Ellis Boerkamp, Flora Haaijer-Ruskamp, Jan Reuyl and Albert Versluis, is concerned with the decision-making process of physicians and reports on empirical research. Technical and process dimensions significantly relate to the

---

* Kunst, P. and J. Lemmink (eds.), 1992, *Quality Management in Services*, Assen: Van Gorcum, and Kunst, P. and J. Lemmink (eds.), 1995, *Managing Service Quality*, QMS, Vol. 1, London: Paul Chapman Publishing Ltd./Vught: Jacques G.M. Hendrikx Innovation Trading B.V.

disconfirmation with an information supplier. Expertise plays an important role in cases where a professional customer evaluates service quality.

Chapter 3, by Harriëtte Greve, Ruud Frambach and Theo Verhallen, is a description of the client-advisor interaction process with respect to financial advice. The authors arrive at the conclusion that the advice often failed to probe for client wishes, but started with a presentation of alternative product solutions, which is typical of a hard-selling approach.

Chapter 4, by Frédéric Marion, studies customer participation in two organisations and tries to relate this to satisfaction.

Richard Varey and Colin Gilligan wrote Chapter 5 on internal marketing. Their contribution focuses on the role of internal marketing with respect to inter-facing the internal and external environments.

The book concludes with three chapters on the measurement of service quality. In the past ten years, the Service Quality Model (SERVQUAL) played a dominant role. Academics and practitioners increasingly comment on the model and the way quality is measured. However, up until now, there has been no indication that a new or alternative model has been developed including the same rich research spin-off.

In chapter 6, Michèle Paulin and Jean Perrien question the concept of SERVQUAL on the basis of a literature review. They conclude that future studies must take into account the effect of contextuality. Jozée Lapierre and Pierre Filiatrault suggest, in Chapter 7, new measurement dimensions in applications to professional services. Finally, in Chapter 8, Uolevi Lehtinen, Jukka Ojasalo and Katri Ojasalo replicated on a small-scale the basic SERVQUAL research in which the service quality dimensions were developed. In cases of simple services, they arrived at a different dimensional structure, indicating that SERVQUAL is not the unique and valid solution to service quality measurement problems.

This series of workshops on Managing Service Quality is becoming increasingly mature. This maturity is reflected by the organisation of the workshops and the cooperation of workshop organisers to the editing process. In 1994, Audrey Gilmore and David Carson, who organised the Paris workshop, made a great contribution in this respect. They helped us to select the papers, and on their initiative, for the first time we also used evaluation forms, filled in by the workshop participants, in the review process.

Gerry van Dijck, programme director of EIASM, also played an important role. Her continued support for the workshops is of great value to our attempts to improve the state of the art.

Publishing books without publishers is a hazardous adventure. Therefore, we thank Paul Chapman (Publishing Ltd) for his efforts to publish this volume, and Jacques Hendrikx (Innovation Trading B.V.) for his help to further develop this series of books.

Finally, we would like to thank Corien Gijsbers at MERIT for her assistance in typesetting and copyediting this book. Without her, we would have been unable to deliver such service to the authors, or a book with such an appealing layout. In other words: the process quality outcome was mainly her work!

Maastricht, October 1995

Paul Kunst and Jos Lemmink

Table of Contents

CHAPTER 8
On Service Quality Models, Service Quality Dimensions and Customers'
Perceptions
Uolevi Lehtinen, Jukka Ojasalo and Katri Ojasalo

Curricula Vitae

Ellis Boerkamp studied economics at the University of Groningen, The Netherlands, specialising in business administration and more specifically services marketing. After completing her studies in 1990, she was appointed as a doctoral candidate in Services Marketing at the Faculty of Economics in Groningen. Her thesis is concerned with the marketing of professional services in hospitals and is due to be completed in the first half of 1995. Recently, she joined Science & Strategy, a marketing consulting company located at Utrecht, concentrating on services marketing and research. Her main research interests are in service quality, consumer satisfaction and relationship marketing.

Andrea Bonaccorsi is Assistant Professor of Marketing at the University of Pisa, Italy. His research interests include: management of innovation, theories of contracts and decision theory. He has published in the *Journal of International Business Studies*, *Journal of International Marketing*, *Journal of Industrial Marketing Management*, and the *Journal of Product Innovation Management*.

Anna Fiorentino is a doctoral student of Marketing at the Scuola Superiore S. Anna in Pisa, Italy. She has a Master's degree in Management of Innovation. Her research interests are: customer satisfaction, services marketing, consumer behaviour, decision theory.

Pierre Filiatrault, Eng. Ph.D., is Professor of Marketing at the École des Sciences de la Gestion of the Université du Québec à Montréal. He is the author and co-author of books and chapters of books including *Le management du marketing* and Marketing bancaire: Services aux consommateurs and of numerous articles in the *Journal of Consumer Research*, *The Journal of Psychology*, *The Journal of Social Psychology*, *International Journal of Bank Marketing*, *Journal of Travel Research*, *Industrial Marketing Management*, *Journal of Professional Services* and others.

Ruud Frambach received his Ph.D. from the Faculty of Economics at Tilburg University, The Netherlands, where he is currently Assistant Professor of Marketing and Marketing Research at the Department of Business Administration. His dissertation was concerned with the diffusion of innovations on the industrial market. His current research interests include the adoption and diffusion of innovations and the formulation and implementation of marketing strategy.

Colin Gilligan is Professor of Marketing at the Sheffield Business School, Sheffield Hallam University, Sheffield, UK.

Harriëtte Greve is a Ph.D. student in Marketing and Marketing Research at the Department of Business Administration of Tilburg University, The Netherlands. Her dissertation research focuses on personal advice in financial services. Her current research interest include personal selling, consultative selling and services marketing.

Flora Haaijer-Ruskamp is Professor in drug utilisation studies with a special interest in the decision-making process of physicians, at the University of Groningen, The Netherlands. She participates in the research programmes of GUIDE (Groningen Utrecht Institute of Drug Exploration) and NCH (Northern Centre of Health Care Research). She is the international coordinator of a European network supported by BIOMED/EU.

Paul Kunst studied business administration at the Erasmus University in Rotterdam, the Free University in Amsterdam, and the University of Amsterdam, Netherlands, where he graduated in 1983. From 1983 until 1989 he was an Assistant Professor at the Faculty of Economics and Business Administration, University of Limburg, Maastricht. He has been involved in studies concerned with works councils, as well as studies on the relations between strategy, structure, culture and control. Paul Kunst is now a consultant and part-time senior research fellow at MERIT, where his main research interest concentrates on quality management, management accounting and human resource management.

Jozée Lapierre is Assistant Professor of High-Technology Marketing at École Polytechnique de Montréal. In 1993, she received her Ph.D. (honours) in management, specialising in industrial marketing, from Université du Québec à Montréal. Her main research interests are the evaluation of technical professional services and the commercialisation of new technologies. She teaches courses on the commercialisation of new technologies and on aspects of industrial innovation at the B.A., Master's and Ph.D. levels.

Uolevi Lehtinen is Professor of Marketing at the University of Tampere. His fields of expertise are services marketing, international marketing and marketing decision making. He has published more than one hundred scientific publications and lectured in twenty countries. He has also been an entrepreneur and consultant.

Jos Lemmink studied business administration at the University of Groningen and was employed at the Head Office of the Dutch Postal Services and Telecommunication in The Hague for four years. He is now Associate Professor of Marketing at the University of Limburg. He has been involved in studies concerned with measurement methods and techniques in marketing pricing strategies and distribution channels studies. His research focuses on the competitive effects of product quality improvements and measuring service quality, and, in general, quality management in services.

Frédéric Marion is a research fellow in service management at the Institut de Recherche de l'Entreprise (IRE), the research centre of the Lyon Graduate School of Business, France. Since he joined the service company management research team at the IRE, Frédéric Marion has carried out research on service processes, service quality and customer participation.

Jukka Ojasalo is a researcher at the Finnish Center for Service and Relationship Management in the Swedish School of Economics and Business Administration in Helsinki. He has also worked in several managerial and consultancy positions in the Finnish industry and public sector.

Katri Ojasalo is a researcher at the Finnish Center for Service and Relationship Management in the Swedish School of Economics and Business Administration in Helsinki.

Michèle Paulin has a law degree from the Université de Sherbrooke, and an Executive MBA degree from the Concordia University in Montréal. She also has considerable managerial experience in the retail business. At present, she is completing her doctoral study in Administration (marketing) at the Université du Québec à Montréal (UQAM). Her dissertation involves the study of relationship marketing in the commercial banking industry within the context of the North American Free Trade Agreement (NAFTA).

Jean Perrien is a Professor at the Université du Québec à Montréal, Canada. He holds a doctorate from the Catholic University of Louvain, Belgium. For some eight years he has been involved in research on services marketing and more precisely on relationship marketing, as applied to services. As a consultant he has been actively involved in the development and training of Canadian bankers on behalf of the Institute of Canadian Bankers and Canadian financial institutions.

Jan Reuyl is Professor of Services Marketing at the Economics faculty, University of Groningen, The Netherlands. His publications include a number of books and articles in, for example, the *Journal of Marketing* and the *Journal of Marketing Research*.

Richard Varey is Director of the BNFL Corporate Communication Unit of The Management School, University of Salford, UK.

Theo Verhallen has held the position of Professor in Marketing and Marketing Research at the Department of Business Administration and CentER at Tilburg University since 1991. He studied economics and psychology, and was associate professor in economic psychology until 1985. He then became the research director of Research International in Rotterdam, as from 1988 combined with a research professorship in marketing research at Tilburg University. His publications include articles in the *Journal of Economic Psychology* and the *Journal of Consumer Research* on marketing research methodology and consumer psychology.

Albert Versluis graduated as a pharmacist in 1972 at the University of Groningen, The Netherlands. From 1972 until 1976 he was a fellow at the Scientific Council of Nuclear Power and he specialised in nuclear pharmacy at the Department of Nuclear Medicine, University Hospital Groningen. In 1977 he was registered as a hospital pharmacist and he became a member of the Hospital Pharmacy staff at the same hospital. In 1984 he was appointed director of pharmacy. His main interests are in pharmaco-epidemiology, information sciences, and marketing of internal services.

1

Customer Service Satisfaction in Market and Intra-Company Exchanges

Andrea Bonaccorsi[1] and Anna Fiorentino[2]

This article discusses customer satisfaction in service exchanges performed by a unit of a large multidivisional firm, within organisational boundaries (internal customers) and across them (market relationships). It is argued that the comparative static analysis of transactions carried out between and inside organisations is based on the untenable assumption that markets and hierarchies do not differ in qualitative terms in the way they coordinate economic transactions, but only because of their associated costs. The argument is put forward that the hypothesis of qualitative heterogeneity has a larger explanatory power in the comparison of the effectiveness of the two governance mechanisms. The discussion is based on an empirical analysis of the case of IBM Semea in Italy.

Introduction

The development of the concepts of *internal customer* and *internal marketing* in large profit organisations has led, in recent years, to the application of customer satisfaction concepts, methodologies and techniques to the analysis and measurement of intra-organisational exchanges. In most situations, the box of tools offered in the customer satisfaction literature and practice has been applied to intra-organisational exchanges with no substantial modification, while no theoretical argument has been put forward on the homogeneity between customer relations in market and in organisational contexts.

It is our contention that the concepts and techniques developed for the analysis of market customer satisfaction *cannot* be applied to the internal customer. To develop this theme, we will try to integrate streams of literature from the economics of organisations, on the one hand, and the customer satisfaction tradition in marketing, on the other.

So far, very little attention has been given in the literature to the relationship between customer choice and satisfaction, and the institutional context in which

---

1   Assistant Professor of Marketing, University of Pisa, Italy.
2   Doctoral student of marketing, Scuola Superiore S. Anna, Pisa, Italy.

choice and satisfaction take place. We argue that this situation depends on strong underlying assumptions that are held in both research fields. In consumer choice theory, the theory of rational decision, which underlies most of the literature on additive satisfaction functions, explicitly states that preferences, and hence satisfaction, are *context-independent*.

On the other hand, mainstream economics of organisations in both the neo-classical and neo-institutional traditions is based on the assumption that markets and hierarchies do not differ in qualitative terms in the way they coordinate economic transactions, but only because of their associated costs. We will challenge these assumptions and develop an alternative integrative framework. We will use empirical material to illustrate our argument, taken from a field study at IBM Semea in Italy.

In this article we discuss customer satisfaction in service exchanges performed by the same organisational unit within organisational boundaries (internal customers) and across them (market exchanges). We considered the relationships existing between this unit of a large multidivisional firm, and internal and external customers supplying software and consulting on business process models. We analysed customer satisfaction with these services, and the nature of the two relationships. The most interesting aspect is that external customers have been found to exhibit significantly higher levels of satisfaction, in surveys conducted from 1991 to 1993.

As will be shown, this result is in sharp contrast with the traditional transaction cost approach in determining when organisations are efficient in coordinating economic exchanges.

The article is structured as follows: the first part introduces the problems of quality evaluation and customer satisfaction in the field of services. In the second part, we will discuss the neo-institutional approach to the analysis of transaction costs generated by service exchanges, and we will show the relationship between the levels of customer satisfaction and transaction costs. This will be followed by the empirical findings. In the last part of the article, an alternative explanation will be proposed to explain the results.

Service Quality Perception and Satisfaction

Intangibility is probably the main characteristic of services, which affects production, sale, quality perceptions and customer satisfaction. It matters for customers because it makes it difficult, and sometimes impossible, to evaluate service quality before purchasing it. In many cases it is difficult also after purchase and use. Zeithaml [1981] has examined the different evaluation processes a consumer adopts towards services and products, referring to three 'groups' of quality characteristics that can be found, in different proportions, both in product and in services. They are classified as *search quality, experience quality, credence quality*.

Search quality is represented by attributes that customers may see, feel or touch, and thus evaluate prior to purchasing the good.

Experience quality is composed of the attributes that may be evaluated after purchase, and during or after consumption, such as respondence to requirements or assistance.

Credence quality is made of all those elements that customers may find diffi-cult to evaluate even after purchase or use. These are intangible elements whose judgement of quality is strictly related to, for example, reliability, attention of the company for the customer, the confidence that the supplier acts in the customer's interest, which are all reflected in the organisation's credibility. It is difficult to evaluate this type of attributes because judgement is influenced by subjective per-ceptions and feelings, and is variable over time. As experience and credence qual-ity dominate in services, because intangibility does not allow customers to evalu-ate physical attributes prior to purchase, the evaluation process adopted with ser-vices is different from that used for goods, in which search quality is far more im-portant. Therefore, the perception of quality in services is also related, to some ex-tent, to the 'relational' aspect of the exchange, i.e., the supplier's credibility and re-liability. Thus, a large amount of the judgement of quality is related to, and de-pends on, the climate of the relationship and on the trust the company builds with its customers, giving them the idea they are being 'treated fairly'.

The Costs Stemming from Service Transactions

The intrinsic difficulty in evaluating the quality of services gives origin to per-formance and evaluation ambiguity [Bowen and Jones, 1986], which in turn raise transaction costs.

Ambiguity stems from the difficulties of the parties to objectively measure all the elements involved in the exchange, and, even after measurement, to evaluate their quality. Ambiguity is mainly derived from a complexity of the object ex-changed in the transaction, for which it is difficult to ascertain both inputs and outputs in the transformation process, and the quality level.

As the traditional transaction cost approach states, a necessary (although insuf-ficient) condition for a perfect functioning of the market is the certainty of the value of the parties' performances, because the perception of equity that rules ex-changes is based on this evaluation process. On the contrary, a performance that is subject to difficulties in evaluation, as in services, affects the possibility to objec-tively state an equity condition. It might allow opportunistic behaviours to the parties of the transaction, which might attempt to overestimate the value and cost of the performance, or the resources necessary to its accomplishment, taking ad-vantage of a condition of information asymmetry.

The main variable that causes performance ambiguity in service exchanges is intangibility. As the degree of intangibility increases, the difficulties of users to evaluate the exchange increase, because there exists less concrete 'proof' to deter-mine the quality level of the service received. Due to this aspect, as stated above, in service exchanges the attributes of credence quality are particularly important; they are based on the feelings of trust that the supplier builds in its customers over time, because the latter might not have sufficient knowledge to evaluate whether or not the service effectively responds to their needs, even after purchase (for ex-ample, in consulting services, customers might not have sufficient knowledge to judge the supplier's output). Without this feeling of reliability, in the attempt to determine the value of the counterpart's offer in the exchange, the buyer could be forced to search for additional information. In market exchanges, the buyer could try to contact many potential suppliers prior to choosing, in order to obtain an ob-jective value of the service. This forces customers to bear 'information search' costs, which are a kind of transaction costs. At times, buyers might be also forced to make post-purchase evaluations: while with physical goods they can easily collect information prior to purchase, with services they might be having difficulty trying to find concrete proof of the quality to be delivered, because what they often obtain is only a 'promise'. As a consequence, they might engage in post-purchase monitoring activities, to check to see if contractual agreements have been respected. Moreover, it is possible that the buyer's awareness of an information asymmetry about service quality might increase the customer's perception of the risk that the transaction is not being carried out in a reciprocity condition. The situation of *'information impactedness'* between the parties implies that a correct evaluation of service quality and equity of transactions is possible only in the long term. In order to reduce these information search costs, customers try to establish long-term relationships with a single supplier, if they believe that these relationships are fair.

In sum, performance ambiguity in services is a major source of transaction costs. The bigger the problems with evaluation, the bigger the difficulties to balance the value of the performances of the parties, the more costly it will be to negotiate, enforce, and monitor service exchanges. This also entails that the more complex should be the transaction governance mechanisms, due to the possible emergence of appropriable quasi-rents. In traditional transaction cost economics, "...if opportunities to appropriate quasi-rents from a particular specialised investment arise frequently, then contracting parties may find it economical to craft a specialised governance structure to deal with these temptations" [Klein, Crawford and Alchian, 1978].

Hence, in the traditional transaction cost approach, the exchanges of highly intangible services, with related problems of information impactedness, would receive considerable advantages from their coordination inside an organisation. This might allow for the exploitation of a number of favourable conditions inside the firm, such as goal congruence [Bowen and Jones, 1986] and the opportunities to overcome performance ambiguity, thanks to the strict relationships between the parties, many informal opportunities and an idiosyncratic, common language. Thus, organisations may be considered more efficient also in the sense that they allow the customer to better perceive and assess service quality before purchase as well. Furthermore, internal organisation creates the context for balancing the evaluation of repeated service exchange over a long-term horizon, thus reducing the impact of the perception of unfairness in single episodes. In other words, for any given level of (service) production costs, the higher the performance and evaluation ambiguity, the higher the transaction costs, the more probable is the integration of service production in a common ownership governance structure.

Finally, an integrative argument for the superiority of internal exchange of services over market exchange can be found in the service marketing literature. According to many authors, for example, the participation of users in the process of production of services is one of the key elements for customer satisfaction. The user of a service can appreciate the effort of a service producer, have a better understanding of its organisation and operations, and provide accurate information on his/her requirements. Again, the involvement of users in the design and delivery of services should be easier within organisational boundaries, given a common culture and language, congruence of goals, frequent informal opportunities of contact. In hierarchical transactions, the firm's top managers can encourage the buyer's involvement in the production process, stimulating integration between the parties and the formation of teams. Internal customers can be requested to cooperate, so as to develop personal long-term relationships in which both parties can act to overcome the problem of performance ambiguity. Mainly on the customer's part, this can be a means to better evaluate experience and credence quality of highly intangible services. Above all, there would be many favourable conditions to reaffirm goal congruence between the parties, and the fact that the supplier acts in the customer's interest.

Does Customer Satisfaction Affect Transaction Costs?

As mentioned previously, transaction cost analysis focuses on the functioning of the governance mechanisms of transactions and on their ability to rule the exchanges in an efficient, but chiefly equitable, way. In fact, the foundation of all exchanges is that the transaction is carried out in a condition of reciprocity, so that the value of the respective performances is fair. This is the main reason why contracting, enforcing and monitoring costs arise. In synthesis, a transaction cost is every activity undertaken to ensure to the parties of an exchange the equivalence of the performances. This reciprocity condition is also mentioned in the traditional marketing literature: Bagozzi [1975] speaks of an "equitable exchange" as the fundamental element of economic relationships.

In this part of the analysis we will show how transaction costs can be affected by the level of customer satisfaction reached in an exchange, and why this can be considered as an indicator of how well a governance mechanism assures equitable exchanges.

Disconfirmation of expectations and *equity* are the two main theoretical paradigms that can be considered to show the bond between customer satisfaction and transaction costs.

The first paradigm implies that satisfaction is a function of the difference between expectations concerning the performance of the service or product to be purchased, as formulated before purchase, and the subsequent perception of this performance, after purchase and use. Satisfaction arises when perceived performance meets or exceeds expectations.

Five main dimensions of satisfaction have been found to be determinant in the literature on service quality [Parasuraman, Zeithaml, Berry, 1988] and to affect customer satisfaction through the comparison of the perceived performance with previous expectations. They are *tangibles, empathy, responsiveness, reliability, assurance*. Hence, as can be seen, customer satisfaction is strictly related to the *relational* aspects of the exchange. For instance, the last two dimensions are defined, respectively, as "the ability to perform the *promised* service dependably and accurately", and "knowledge and courtesy of employees and their ability *to inspire trust and confidence*"[3]. So customers formulate expectations about the fact that they can trust the counterpart, and that the exchange will guarantee equity to the parties. Satisfaction towards these two elements has non-trivial effects on the costs that the parties bear to self-guarantee a reciprocity in the contractual exchange. If

---

3   The emphasis does not appear in the original text.

in the customer's experience there is an unwavering feeling of satisfaction with these aspects (essentially regarding the supplier), he will have a positive attitude towards the subsequent exchanges. The expectation of compliance of the other party reduces the costs of enforcing and monitoring, and lowers the risks of information impactedness. This confidence allows for the adoption of less complex contractual mechanisms, and thus for spending fewer resources in the definition of clauses that protect against non-fulfilment or opportunistic behaviours.

If we take into account the second paradigm of customer satisfaction based on the notion of 'equity', the link with transaction costs is even more immediate. In this approach, the main determinant of customer satisfaction is the perception of *fairness* of the exchange. We adopt here the concept of equity proposed by Oliver and Swan [1989], which takes into account a definition of satisfaction that includes an evaluation of both parties' outcomes in the judgement of satisfactory exchanges, rather than only the buyer's perceived performance of the service delivered, as opposed to previous expectations. In this perspective, a building block of the buyer's overall satisfaction with the transaction is the perception (and evaluation) of the counterpart's outcomes from the exchange. The judgement of fairness is given when the input/outcome ratio for the parties involved in the exchange is considered equal. However, this concept needs further explanation. Oliver and Swan have distinguished the definition of equity in commercial exchanges from the concept of 'equal partners', used in the social exchange perspective. Instead, they have adopted the viewpoint of different roles for the parties, which relies on the concept of 'distributive justice'. This framework is very suitable in the context of sales transactions, where customer and supplier are expected to perform different roles. The theory [Berger, Conner and Hamit Frisek, 1974] prescribes that each party of a transaction has expectations about the other's role. So equity, or justice, is interpreted in terms of the other's performance, as compared to a certain role expected. When one party has the idea that the other is not acting his role, thus lowering his input/output ratio, a feeling of inequity may arise. If one party perceives a risk of inequity in the transaction, there could be a higher demand for sophisticated contractual agreements that ensure protection, thus raising the costs of contracting, monitoring and enforcing.

The Customer Satisfaction Surveys at IBM Semea

We use empirical material from a case study to support our contention that customer satisfaction is not independent of the institutional context in which the exchange takes place. In the period May-July 1992 we carried out a series of in-depth interviews with managers and had access to internal files of the division 'Information Process' of IBM Semea in Italy. A follow-up to the field survey was carried out in 1993 and January 1994.

Following a major restructuring of internal organisation and the adoption of a corporate policy based on customer orientation, IBM Semea created an 'internal customer' system in 1990. The general philosophy was to shift emphasis from functional specialisation to the management of processes oriented towards the satisfaction of customers, both external and internal.

To monitor the level of satisfaction of internal and external customers, the 'Information Process' division, which delivers software and consulting, carries out an annual Customer Satisfaction Survey. A detailed questionnaire was developed on the basis of the five quality dimensions identified by the SERVQUAL model [Parasuraman *et al.*, 1988]. For example, customers were asked questions relating to their satisfaction with responsiveness, comprehension of exigencies, respondence to requirements, empathy of personnel, goal congruence, professionalism, price.

At the end of the year, internal customers were asked to rate their level of satisfaction over the attributes for the services delivered during that year, while questionnaires were administered to external customers after each service had been provided. The internal surveys were carried out with both end users and the managers of the business units to which the services were delivered. End users received an instrument containing 25 questions, while business unit managers received forms with ten questions. External surveys also contained ten questions. In all questionnaires a five-point scale was used as follows:

1 = completely satisfied,
2 = quite satisfied,
3 = neither satisfied nor dissatisfied,
4 = quite dissatisfied,
5 = completely dissatisfied.

A synthetic final data was calculated, the 'Net Satisfaction Index' (N.S.I.), which is the weighted arithmetic average of the points assigned to the different variables of the Surveys, transformed in a growing 0-100 scale[4] (it may be also expressed in the five-point scale). The data collected are showed in the tables below.

Table 1.1   N.S.I. calculated for internal end users

1991	66,04	(n = 110)
1992	65,50	(n = 150)
1993	59,53	(n = 190)

Only one data is available for Business Unit managers: in 1991 the N.S.I. was 60,61. The number of respondents was 20. In market relationships, the N.S.I. for 1991 was 86 (n = 24).

The survey methods for market customers changed in 1992, and the data for 1992 and 1993 were no longer comparable in a cardinal order with those of 1991. Still, the results remained extremely positive, with a further sharp increase in 1993[5].

---

4   N.S.I.p = 25 * [5 - ($\Sigma_{1,n}$ weight$_i$*point$_i$)/n]
5   With the new scale, the data were:
     1991 = 70 (converted)
     1992 = 71
     1993 = 80.

In the tables below, we report some details of the points assigned to the different areas surveyed in 1991 by internal business unit managers and external customers[6].

Table 1.2   *Internal customer satisfaction results*
(Source: IBM Semea 1992)

Goal sharing	53.57
Adequacy of solutions	80
Results obtained	53.57
Technology	64.29
Assistance	66
Impact on user's strategy	58.33
Responsiveness	55
Relationships	60.71
Flexibility	57.14
Price	50

Table 1.3   *External customer satisfaction results*
(Source: IBM Semea 1992)

Objectives reached	84.75
Adequacy of solutions	87.5
Results obtained	79.25
Professionalism	85.75
Quality	86.25
Added value	88
Customer interest	91
Responsiveness	84.25
Relationships	89.25
Competitiveness	68.25

The tables show considerable differences in the dimensions concerning the relational aspect of the exchanges, such as relationships, responsiveness, and interest. These results also indicate that the problems with internal exchanges were not just a matter of technical and professional resources. In sharp contrast to Bowen and Jones' approach [1986], in internal exchanges one of the lowest points was assigned to the supplier's 'goal sharing' with the buyer (the scale of priorities to be reached with the service): this aspect was satisfactory at a level of only 53.57, while it had been given the highest weight.

A similar importance assigned to this element accounts for a strong need of coordination in the supply of services. This may be considered the response to overcoming the problems of intangibility and the difficulty in determining standards of acceptance on which parties can agree without ambiguity. The need for common goals stands for the exigency of customer and supplier being committed to a single and clear objective in order to overcome performance ambiguity.

---

6   We consider the data of this survey more comparable with the data collected with external customers, because the items were more similar and because the questionnaires were in both cases completed by unit managers rather than end users.

Another data worth noting is that personal relationships between the parties scored, in internal exchanges, only 60.71 while with external customers it was 89.25. Moreover, during personal interviews carried out after the survey had taken place, internal customers clearly expressed dissatisfaction with the supplier personnel, who often had an arrogant attitude. These results are interesting for different reasons.

First, the results of IBM Semea's *Customer Satisfaction Surveys*, carried out in 1991, 1992 and 1993 with internal customers and in market exchanges showed a different performance in these two types of transactions, although the nature of services delivered and, often, the salespersons were the same. Following the traditional approach to transaction cost analysis [Bowen and Jones, 1986] and given the high level of intangibility, ambiguity and customisation of the services offered, we would have expected a higher level of satisfaction in internal exchanges. Therefore, it is interesting to explore whether the transaction cost explanation and the customer satisfaction paradigm can clarify these anomalies.

Second, the difference in satisfaction between the internal and external context is higher exactly concerning attributes that should, *a priori*, be favourably affected by the internal governance of the exchange. An observation might concern the fact that internal customers' lower satisfaction might be due to their higher levels of expectations. But according to the theory presented above, there are reasons for internal customers to have *more accurate* expectations, but not *higher*. Thanks to the knowledge of the supplier's delivery processes and the efforts made to achieve the result, the customer may get to know the actual value of the service exchanged and formulate more precise expectations[7].

Irreversibility of Transformation of Resources and the Transaction Costs Explanation

Is the transaction cost approach (TCA) to service exchange a useful tool for the analysis of internal customer satisfaction? How might this approach explain our results?

The analysis of the processes of vertical integration and organisational transformation has been dealt with, in transaction cost economics [Williamson, 1985], as a problem of minimising the sum of production and governance costs. The decision to integrate productive resources, according to transaction cost economics, is based on the comparison of production and transaction costs encountered in using the market, and those encountered in using the firm. Thus, the problem has essentially two facets: technology and coordination. The criterion adopted in choosing the best alternative is minimisation of the sum of these costs.

Therefore, the standard TCA explanation in this case would take into account a typical problem of coordination: incentives. Given the lack of *true* competition for the internal supplier of services, there might be *insufficient incentives for performance*. The same organisational unit might concentrate efforts on the external customer, where the risk of supplier switching might be substantial, while devot-

---

7   Internal customers' higher expectations could be due to higher expected commitment of the supplier. However, this view would entail that internal suppliers have more powerful incentives than external ones. This is in contrast with a large amount of literature that affirms the superiority of market incentives and has led to the conceptualisation of internal marketing.

ing scarce resources to the internal customers. This argument has strong roots in the idea of *powered* incentives proposed by Williamson [1985]. According to Williamson, market competition provides the *strongest* incentive for performance, while hierarchical incentives are less powerful although highly effective given their selective nature.

However, if these arguments were true, the difference between market and internal customer would be simply based on the degree of *actual* competition. If a large company really abolished any corporate mandate to 'buy inside', then there would be, in principle, no difference in the structure of incentives. This does not seem to be the case. In the IBM Semea case we analysed, the corporate policy for internal procurement of services was to allow for complete freedom of choice. Furthermore, there was no evidence of an unbalance of resource allocation and customer attention between the internal and external customer.

It is important to underline that the TCA explanation is based on the hypothesis of perfect reversibility of the make-or-buy or efficient boundary choice. According to this hypothesis, markets and hierarchies do not differ with respect to the quality of productive resources under governance, but only with respect to the associated transaction costs. Productive resources do not undergo any qualitative transformation when moving across organisational boundaries. The theory does not clarify any qualitative difference. But the pure transactional approach, indirectly, assumes another strong implication, which is the perfect reversibility or substitutability of the two governance mechanisms. This assumption is necessary to sustain that *transaction costs* determine the boundaries between markets and firms.

Therefore, in this perspective, it is completely appropriate to conceptualise or measure customer satisfaction in the same way, either externally and internally. We go even further by arguing that in the empirical case there was a difference in the way the two relationships were conducted, and a difference in the nature of the services delivered, which could not be completely explained by the traditional transaction cost economics.

Recent developments in the theory of the firm, organisational learning and economics of knowledge and innovation give a richer account of the problem of organisational boundaries. Taken together, these contributions ignore the centrality of equilibrium[8] in economic analysis and stress the role of tacit, idiosyncratic, local and imperfect knowledge in economic processes and exchanges. In this view, market failure arguments are not sufficient to explain organisational boundaries. It is the nature of knowledge, and, in particular, the high cost and imperfectness of transferring knowledge, that dictate organisational forms.[9] As Kogut and Zander [1993, pp. 627] put it: "firms are social communities that serve as efficient mechanisms for the creation and transformation of knowledge into economically rewarded products and services (...). The design of the governance mechanism is not equivalent to the capabilities of firms and what individuals know how to do. Cooperation within an organisation leads to a set of capabilities that are easier to

---

8   None of the authors on the growth of knowledge mentioned here (Loasby, 1986) seem to think that the concept of an equilibrium approach to knowledge is worth considering, unless it produces a concept of disequilibrium as a trigger to action.
9   The cornerstone of the evolutionary theory of the firm is of course Nelson and Winter (1982), who built upon the idea of personal knowledge by M. Polany (1962). On the nature of knowledge and the problem of knowledge transfer, see Teece (1977), Kogut and Zander (1992, 1993).

transfer within the firm than across organisations and constitute the ownership advantage of the firm".

A key point in this view of the firm is that *productive resources change in their nature with use and become increasingly specific*. A similar point is made by Foray [1990], who stresses how the integration of resources within an organisation (integration) reduces the opportunity for trading the same resources in the market (substitutability) as they become more specific.

The analysis of vertical integration of the R&D function by Foray and Mowery [1990] based on the concept of absorptive capacity [Cohen and Levinthal, 1988] is also relevant to our discussion. According to these authors, when R&D is integrated in the organisation, and as the organisation develops over time, this function changes in nature and becomes increasingly 'organisation-specific'. In other words, a qualitative transformation occurs, and the above-mentioned hypothesis of reversibility falls, due to this change in its nature. Mainly, it develops, along with its peculiar function of innovation, a capacity of learning that it could not obtain in market exchanges. Vertical integration, through the association of different functions and conjoint use, entails a change in the nature of these resources. The traditional theory of vertical integration ignores the effects of the development of tacit, idiosyncratic knowledge through personal interrelationships.

From this initial point of view, we have extended the concept of qualitative heterogeneity of internal transactions. We argue that, when transactions are carried out inside organisations, they go through irreversible transformations that no longer provide viable exit options for the parties.

If in the traditional approach it is sustained that a condition of substitutability of the resources is implicit, it is also held that the parties maintain the option to 'exit', i.e., to abandon the relationship and move to another counterpart[10]. It is also believed that maintaining an exit option for the parties, inside an organisation, is a necessary condition to hypothesise that the market's high-powered incentives may work inside the organisation. Anyway, this opportunity, in certain situations, is not able to prevent the parties from the holdup risks.

The decision to bring inside the organisation the activities that satisfy internal exigencies leads, as a consequence, to the creation of highly transaction-specific investments, as they are created to produce output for a single customer. So the relationship between customer and supplier is strongly idiosyncratic. But a holdup condition does not merely stem from the emergence of specialised assets. It derives from the transformation that the specialised assets went through since their integration, and from then, through the development of the organisation. The conjoint use of specialised resources determines transaction-specific processes in the delivery of services. This creates an idiosyncratic exchange of competencies that leads to the development of a tacit and unique knowledge for both parties. The development of these intangible, exchange-specific resources determine non-substitutability of the parties with others and non-reversibility of the investments, because they are no longer equal to those in the market. Hence, in spite of the existence of a formal possibility of exit (as in IBM), this option is made not viable by the transformation of the nature of the transaction. Thus, the conjoint use of the

---

10 A classical formulation of this exit option, even *within* the organisation, is given by Alchian and Demsetz [1972].

crucial resources of a transaction determines a sort of mutual dependence of the parties to the exchange.

Internal Post-Contractual Opportunism and Power

A holdup condition generates a disequilibrium in the position of the two parties. In particular, it allows the supplier to achieve a monopoly condition that can be accompanied by opportunistic behaviour aimed at strengthening this position inside the organisation. Thus, our contention is that a holdup condition inside the organisation is generated by the irreversibility of the resources and relationships established between the two parties. This is due to an intangible set of personal, tacit knowledge and competencies that are absolutely peculiar to this exchange, whose specificity increases as the organisation develops through time.

The emergence of a holdup condition allows the supplier to obtain a monopoly power that increases as the specificity of these intangible resources increase, thus allowing for a sort of post-contractual opportunism.

Several authors refer to the possibilities of opportunistic behaviours inside an organisation.

Williamson [1985] and Walker and Poppo [1991] argue that organisations tend to maintain authority over internal transactions, regardless the level of asset specificity. This may lead to corporate encouragement to buy inside, mainly as a means to reach economies of scale. If we consider the credibility of the threats of exit for the parties, this lowers the expectation to terminate the relationship, further weakening the position of the buyer. In fact, if the transactions are to be maintained, they will probably establish a situation in which the supplier has captive customers. In captive markets, the incentives for the supplier to perform according to the customer's expectations is fairly limited, given that customer satisfaction and judgement do not have 'the last word'. Furthermore, there is less attention for the use of results and suggestions arising from internal surveys. The supplier-customer relationship, in fact, is not flexibly adapted for increasing customer satisfaction, but depends on predefined organisational variables.

In our case, services delivered by the internal unit during one year are planned in advance in order to saturate productive capacity; the internal transfer price is based on direct costs and is not sensitive to perceived service quality and customer satisfaction.

Therefore, neither the volume of demand to meet, nor the price level, are influenced by customer feedback. This is to say that the internal supplier who takes advantage of a holdup condition and has captive customers may have a low incentive to perform well. The strong implication of this analysis is that a formal exit option is a necessary but not sufficient condition to guarantee that in internal transactions the incentive properties of the market can be maintained. This point is also consistent with the analysis of different forms of post-contractual opportunism. Internal organisation can reduce transaction costs arising from the holdup problem, but is not effective, in itself, against cheating [Franzini, 1994]. In sum, given the organisation's internal procurement bias, a potential supplier's post-contractual opportunistic behaviour could be strengthened.

The problem of *influence costs* [Milgrom and Roberts, 1990] is also worth mentioning, which are associated with "centralised, discretionary decision-making power inherent in formal economic organisations such as firms". These costs arise from individuals seeking to influence the organisation's decisions for their private benefit, and from the organisation's responses to this behaviour. Those who have discretionary authority may misuse it to achieve personal goals, or may attempt to persuade others to use authority in their interest. Thus, influence costs arise first because individuals and groups within the organisation spend time and effort while attempting to affect other people's decisions for their benefit, and secondly because inefficient decisions result either directly from these influence activities or, less directly, from attempts to prevent or control them.

One reason why the risks of influence are always present in organisations is that top management's decisions depend heavily upon information, which is often not available to them directly. Hence, they must rely upon others, with the risk of a voluntary distortion of information by employees who try to reach private objectives. As regards the empirical case, it is worth stressing the importance of information in service exchanges, as explained above, as regards quality and the resources necessary for their production.

Perception of Inequity and Dissatisfaction

In our case, the tendency to reinforce the monopoly for the supplier was revealed by the fact that, against the users' expectations, the services were highly technology-based and the software was not very user-friendly. This often entailed difficulties in the comprehension and ease of use for the customers.

Even if it was very difficult to demonstrate, due to their condition of information impactedness, customers had the feeling that the type of services the supplier usually delivered was aimed at reinforcing the situation of idiosyncratic structures and relations. This was proved by the creation of complex computer networks having a high level of hardware and software integration, with a strong need for continuous assistance. This specificity increased the strength of the position and the advantages acquired by the supplier as a first mover.

On the customer's side, the perception of the different relative power of the parties may be a reason for dissatisfaction, because it can be felt as an obstacle to equitable transactions. This conflict may alter the perceived service quality, because these evaluations are affected by customer dissatisfactions relative to the established relationship and the lack of assurance and reliability. In fact, in IBM the perception of the supplier's attempts to strengthen its monopoly has affected the judgement about the quality of the services and the points assigned in the surveys. In other words, dissatisfaction with the relationship between the parties has been expressed through a low evaluation of the quality of the object exchanged.

Conclusions

Hierarchical transaction may sometimes find a limit in attempting to substitute market relationships. This limit can be revealed by a loss of efficiency in exchanges, which in our case is represented by lower customer satisfaction. This lack of efficiency can derive from the organisational context, namely imperfect substitutability of the parties in exchange, and from a situation of dependence of one of them, which gives rise to opportunistic behaviours. As shown above, even if inside an organisation the parties are allowed a formal possibility of exit, this option is made not viable by the emergence of exchange-specific, non-replaceable resources.

The institutional context seems, then, an important dimension in evaluating and surveying customer satisfaction. It entails a set of relational and organisational attributes of the exchange that should be taken into account when asking the customer about his level of satisfaction. In internal transactions, customers might feel dissatisfied with the *way* the relation takes place, due to organisational variables.

Hence, another observation can be made concerning the tools applied to survey customer satisfaction, and the adequacy of the methodologies used for market exchanges to accurately assess *internal* customer satisfaction. Further research is needed to develop a methodology for internal customer studies that focuses on both the *object* exchanged in the transaction and the *effects* produced by the organisational context in which the transaction takes place.

References

Alchian, A. and H. Demsetz, 1972, 'Production, Information Costs, and Economic Organization', *American Economic Review*, 62 (Dec.), pp.777-795.

Alston, L.J. and W. Gillespie, 1989, 'Resource Coordination and Transaction Costs', *Journal of Economic Behavior and Organization*, 11 (1), pp.191-212.

Bagozzi, R.P., 'Marketing as Exchange', 1975, *Journal of Marketing*, 38 (4), pp.32-39.

Berger, J., T.L. Conner and M. Hamit Frisek, 1974, *Expectation States Theory: A Theoretical Research Program*, Cambridge, Winthrop Publishers.

Berry, L.L., A Parasuraman and V. Zeithaml, 1985, 'Quality Counts in Services, Too', *Business Horizons*, 28 (May-June), pp. 44-52.

Berry, L.L., A Parasuraman and V. Zeithaml, 1988, 'The Service-Quality Puzzle', *Business Horizons*, 31 (5), pp.35-43.

Bowen, D.E. and G.R. Jones, 1986, 'Transaction Cost Analysis of Service Organization-Customer Exchange', *Academy of Management Review*, 11 (2), pp.33-45.

Calvo, G.A. and S. Wellisz, 1978, 'Supervision, Loss of Control and the Optimum Size of the Firm', *Journal of Political Economy*, 86 (5), pp.943-952.

Camacho, A., 1991, 'Adaptation Costs, Coordination Costs and Optimal Firm Size', *Journal of Economic Behavior and Organization*, 15, pp.137-150.

Cohen, W. and D. Levinthal, 1988, 'Innovation and Learning: the Two Facets of R&D. Implication for the analysis of R&D Investments', presented at the International Association J.A. Schumpeter, Siena, Italy, May.

De Alessi, L., 1983, 'Property Rights, Transaction Costs, and X-Efficiency: An Essay in Economic Theory', *American Economic Review*, 73 (1), pp.64-81.

Foray, D., 1990, 'Coopération Industrielle et Equilibre Organisationnel de la Firme Innovatrice', presented at "Les Réseaux d'Innovateurs", HEC, Montréal, May.

Foray, D. and D.C. Mowery, 1990, 'L'Intégration de la R&D Industrielle: Nouvelles Perspectives d'Analyse', *Revue Économique*, (3), pp.501-530.

Franzini, M., 1994, 'Post-Contractual Opportunism and the Market', unpublished paper, University of Siena, Italy.

Granovetter, M., 1985, 'Economic Action and Social Structure: The Problem of Embeddedness', *American Journal of Sociology*, 91 (3), pp.481-510.

Grönroos, C., 1984, 'A Service Quality Model and Its Marketing Implications', *European Journal of Marketing*, 18 (4), pp.10-17.

Grönroos, C., 1987, 'A Service-Oriented Approach to the Marketing of Services', *European Journal of Marketing*, 12 (8), pp.25-36.

Hirschmann, A.O., 1970, *Exit, Voice and Loyalty*, Cambridge, Mass.: Harvard University Press.

Holmstrom, B.R. and J. Tirole, 1989, 'The Theory of the Firm', in R. Schmalensee and R. Willig (eds.), *Handbook of Industrial Organization*, Elsevier Science Publishers.

Kelley, S.W., J. H. Donnelly, Jr. and S.J. Skinner, 1990, 'Customer Participation in Service Production and Delivery', *Journal of Retailing*, 66 (3), pp.315-335.

Klein, B., R. Crawford and A. Alchian, 1978, 'Vertical Integration, Appropriable Rents, and the Competitive Contracting Process', *Journal of Law and Economics*, 21 (Oct.), pp.297-326.

Klein, B and K.B. Leffler, 1981, 'The Role of Market Forces in Assuring Contractual Performance', *Journal of Political Economy*, 89 (4), pp.615-641.

Kogut, B. and U. Zander, 1992, 'Knowledge of the Firm, Combinative Capabilities and the Replication of Technology', *Organizational Science*, 3, pp.383-397.

Kogut, B. and U. Zander, 1993, 'Knowledge of the Firm and the Evolutionary Theory of the Multinational Corporation', *Journal of International Business Studies*, 24 (4), pp.625-645.

Leblebici, H., 1985, 'Transactions and Organizational Forms: A Re-Analysis', *Organization Studies*, 6 (2), pp.97-116.

Leibenstein, H., 1975, 'Aspects of the X-Efficiency Theory of the Firm', *Bell Journal of Economics*, 6 (6), pp. 580-606.

Milgrom, P. and J. Roberts, 1990, 'Bargaining Costs, Influence Costs and the Organization of Economic Activity', in J.E. Alt and K. A. Shepsle (eds.), *Perspectives on Positive Political Economy*, Cambridge University Press.

Moore, S.A. and B.B. Schlegelmilch, 1991, 'A Proposed Methodology for Examining Inter- and Intra-Organizational Perceptions of Service Quality', paper presented at the 7th I.M.P. Conference, Uppsala, Sweden, 6-8 September.

Nelson, R. and S. Winter, 1982, *An Evolutionary Theory of Economic Change*, Cambridge: Harvard University Press.

North, D.C., 1991, *Institutions, Institutional Change and Economic Performance*, Cambridge University Press.

North, D.C., 1991, 'Institutions', *Journal of Economic Perspectives*, 5 (1), pp.97-112.

Oliver, R.L., J.E. Swan, 1989, 'Consumer Perceptions of Interpersonal Equity and Satisfaction in Transactions: A Field Survey Approach', *Journal of Marketing*, 53, pp.21-35 .

Pagano, U., 1991, 'Property Rights, Asset Specificity, and the Division of Labor under Alternative Capitalist Relations', *Cambridge Journal of Economics*, 15, pp.315-342.

Parasuraman, A., L.L. Berry and V.A. Zeithaml, 1985, 'A Conceptual Model of Service Quality and Its Implications for Future Research', *Journal of Marketing*, 49 (Fall), pp.41-50.

Parasuraman, A., V.A. Zeithaml and L.L. Berry, 1988, 'SERVQUAL: A Multiple-Item Scale for Measuring Consumer Perceptions of Service Quality', *Journal of Retailing*, 64 (Spring), pp.12-40.

Polany, M., 1962, *Personal Knowledge. Towards a Post-Critical Philosophy*, New York: Harper and Row.

Rushton, A. M and D.J. Carson, 1989, 'The Marketing of Services. Managing the Intangibles', *European Journal of Marketing*, 23 (8), pp.23-44.

Shostack, G.L., 1987, 'Service Positioning Through Structural Change', *Journal of Marketing*, January.

Simintiras, A.C and M. Zairi, 1991, 'The Psychological Aspect of Quality and the Role of Personal Selling in the Customer-Supplier Chain', paper presented at the 7th I.M.P. Conference, Uppsala, Sweden, 6-8 September.

Teece, D.J., 1977, 'Technology Transfer by Multinational Firms: the Resource cost of Transferring Technological Know-How', *Economic Journal*, 87 (June), pp.242-261.

Walker, G. and L. Poppo, 1991, 'Profit Centers, Single-Source Suppliers, and Transaction Costs', *Administrative Science Quarterly*, 36, pp.66-87.

Williamson, O.E., 1967, 'Hierarchical Control and Optimum Firm Size', *Journal of Political Economy*, 75 (2), pp.123-138.

Williamson, O.E., 1975, *Markets and Hierarchies. Analysis and Antitrust Implications*, New York, The Free Press, New York.

Williamson, O.E., 1981, 'The Economics of Organization: The Transaction Cost Approach', *American Journal of Sociology*, 87 (3), pp.548-577.

Williamson, O.E., 1985, *The Economic Institutions of Capitalism*, New York: Free Press.

Williamson, O.E., 1989, 'Transaction Cost Economics', in R. Schmalensee and R. Willig (eds.), *Handbook of Industrial Organization*, Amsterdam: Elsevier Science Publishers.

Yarbrough, B.V. and R.M. Yarbrough, 1988, 'The Transactional Structure of the Firm,' *Journal of Economic Behavior and Organization*, 10, pp.1-28.

Zeithaml, V.A., 1981, 'How Consumer Evaluation Process Differ Between Goods and Services', in J.H. Donnelly and W.R. George (eds.),*Marketing of Services*, A.M.A., Chicago, pp.186-190.

Zeithaml, V., L.L. Berry and A. Parasuraman, 1988, 'Communication and Control Processes in the Delivery of Service Quality', *Journal of Marketing*, 52 (April), pp.35-48.

Zeithaml, V.A., A. Parasuraman and L.L. Berry, 1985, 'Problems and Strategies in Services Marketing', *Journal of Marketing*, 49 (Spring), pp.33-46.

2

Estimating the Effects of Services Quality on the Decision-Making Process of Physicians[1]

Ellis JC Boerkamp[2], Flora M Haaijer-Ruskamp[3], Jan C Reuyl[2] and Albert Versluis[4]

This article provides insight into the quality aspects used by physicians to evaluate and select information suppliers for consultation in a complex patient problem. We show that the level of (dis)confirmation with an information supplier strongly corresponds with the influence of these different information suppliers on the decision-making process of physicians. A theoretical framework based on services marketing and consumer behaviour literature is defined. Data collected from a large sample of internists were used to estimate the proposed model empirically. Multiple regression analysis showed that technical and process dimensions significantly relate to the (dis)confirmation with an information supplier. The results were generally favourable to the model's framework of information supplier selection.

Introduction

During the medical treatment of a patient, hospital physicians have to make several decisions. They may be confronted with complex problems in every stage of this process, i.e., the diagnosis, the choice of therapy and the implementation of the therapy. This may be a reason for consulting a personal drug information supplier[5], for example a microbiologist, a (hospital) pharmacist, or the pharmaceutical industry. The aim of this study is to provide insight into how personal drug in-

---

1 The authors are indebted to Dr Jan Roelf Bult for his helpful suggestions and to Harald van Heerde, who performed a number of the analyses reported in this article.
2 University of Groningen, Faculty of Economics, Department of Business Administration and Management Sciences, P.O. Box 800, 9700 AV Groningen, The Netherlands (correspondence).
3 University of Groningen, Northern Centre for Health Care Research/GIDS.
4 University Hospital Pharmacy, Groningen/GIDS.
5 Drug information suppliers are also referred to as 'drug information sources' in the medical literature. Both terms will be used throughout this study.

formation suppliers are selected and used by physicians in hospitals. By developing a theoretical framework to examine the importance of drug information suppliers in the decision-making process of hospital physicians, we focus on concepts developed by Parasuraman, Zeithaml and Berry [1985, 1988] and Grönroos [1990] to determine service quality, and on decision-making theories. We hypothesize that the level of disconfirmation which arises when an information source is consulted, strongly corresponds with the perceived importance of this source in the decision-making process.

Background

A good starting point for describing the decision-making process of physicians is the cycle of medical treatment of a patient, i.e., the stages a patient runs through when having a medical treatment. This is shown in Figure 2.1 for the case of pharmacotherapy.

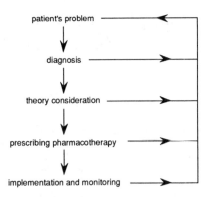

Figure 2.1 Cycle of medical treatment

In this study we will simplify this scheme using a rough classification. We distinguish the following three stages: diagnosis, therapy choice and implementation of the therapy. When confronted with a problem during one of these stages, the physician will search for information to find a solution. Depending on the relevance, recency, and complexity of the problem, either habitual decision making, or internal or external search behaviour will be applied [Denig and Haaijer-Ruskamp, 1992]. We speak of habitual decision making when a choice is made without considering alternatives. Internal search behaviour is used when a physician uses knowledge from memory. When a physician looks for information beyond his own memory we speak of external information search [Hawkins, Best and Coney, 1992].

For external information search, the physician can use a variety of information sources, which can be roughly divided into professional sources and commercial sources. For both categories it is possible to distinguish between personal, written or computerised drug information sources. This is illustrated in Table 2.1.

Table 2.1   Drug information sources of hospital physicians

	Professional sources	Commercial sources
personal	colleagues other medical specialists general practitioners (hospital) pharmacists clinical pharmacologists clinical chemists radiologists microbiologists nurses conferences	industrial representatives conferences
written	journal articles text books compendia formularies	journal articles text books compendia
computerised	databases interactive programs	databases interactive programs

Several authors have given attention to the use of professional and commercial information suppliers [Williams and Hensel, 1991]. These studies vary in size and composition of the sample, the way of data collection, the type of respondents (general practitioners or specialised physicians), and the number of information sources taken into account. The present study is limited to the use of personal drug information suppliers, as we approach this problem field from a services marketing point of view. In sum, we focus on the selection and use of personal drug information suppliers, in the case of external information search of physicians, initiated by a complex patient case during one of the stages of the cycle of medical treatment.

Rationale for the Study

In the 1980s, Parasuraman, Zeithaml and Berry (PZB) presented their well-known Service Quality Model, SERVQUAL [1985, 1988]. It appeared to be an outstanding instrument for measuring quality in service organisations and assessing potential causes of shortfalls in service quality in several service industries, for example banks, telephone companies, repair-and-maintenance services, or credit-card companies. Quality was recognised as an important instrument for developing long-term relationships with satisfied customers. The instrument was also used in the health care sector, mostly to measure patients' evaluations of services offered by hospitals and physicians [Woodside, Frey and Daly, 1989; Reidenbach and Sandifer-Smallwood, 1990; Peyrot, Cooper and Schnapf, 1993]. In the present study we use a modified service quality model to provide insight into the relationships between professional service deliverers in hospitals. We are interested in the criteria that physicians use for the evaluation of professional service providers (the information suppliers) in hospitals. Furthermore, we extend the body of knowledge about service quality and satisfaction by relating these issues to decision-making processes and choice theories.

This study fits in with a trend in health care, in which teams of know-how are created to strive jointly for optimal quality of care. We pay attention to the trend of professionalisation, which can be noticed in some of the health professions. In order to strengthen their position and demarcate their professional domain, a great deal of medical professionals concentrate on improving their expertise and services [Bering, 1992]. Medical physicians have made most progress within this field; they have installed a number of medical-technical criteria, rules of conduct, and profiles of the profession. Although the professionalisation of the paramedical professions is still in its infancy, a lot of them are rapidly catching up. For example, among (hospital) pharmacists a reconsideration of their tasks takes place and they try to expand their role boundaries as members of the medical team [Ortiz, Walker and Thomas, 1989; Boerkamp et al., 1992]. They increasingly want to be viewed as drug information suppliers of physicians[6]. Thus, we gain insight not only into how the information-supplying services of the pharmacist are perceived by physicians, but also how the services of the pharmacist's potential 'competitors' are seen with respect to the quality of the services delivered by them.

A Theory about the Use of Information Sources by Physicians[7]

The above-mentioned research questions are addressed using services marketing literature because, according to the criteria formulated by Gardner [1986], drug information suppliers can be considered professional service suppliers. He defines professional services as advisory services focused on problem solving; they are provided by a qualified person known for specific skills and they include an assignment requested by the client; an independent professional provides this service, supervised by an association which attempts to lay down requirements of competence and to enforce a code of ethics.

For drug information suppliers willing to position themselves as advisors of physicians and nurses, such as (hospital) pharmacists, it is important to know how their clients perceive their services and what their expectations are. Due to the typical characteristics of services, however, it is difficult to gain insight into how clients evaluate service quality and satisfaction. As opposed to goods, services are intangible; very often the client is involved in the production process; and the service is a result of direct interaction between client and supplier [Lovelock, 1991].

To understand service quality and satisfaction, the SERVQUAL model has been shown to be useful [PZB, 1988, Grönroos, 1984]. This approach is based on the disconfirmation paradigm which suggests that both client and supplier need to have consistent expectations and evaluations for a successful service exchange to occur [Oliver, 1980][8].

Applying this to our study leads to the following. When confronted with a complex patient case in a certain stage of the cycle of treatment, the physician, as a professional client, can choose to consult one or more personal drug information

---

6   In fact, (hospital) pharmacists want to disseminate and evaluate information about drugs to all those concerned, including the general public, patients, physicians, nurses, and other health professionals [Hitchings, 1989].

7   This section is based on Boerkamp et al., [1993a]. In this paper, a mathematical derivation of the model can be found.

8   An extensive explanation and discussion of the SERVQUAL approach is given in, for example: ZPB [1990], Carman [1990], Cronin and Taylor [1992].

sources, professional suppliers, on the basis of past expectations and experiences[9]. The information and service finally received by the physician can, however, deviate from his initial expectations. In case of a large discrepancy we speak of a large disconfirmation. We define *disconfirmation* as the positive or negative difference between perceptions and expectations, and *confirmation* as the match between perceptions and expectations [Oliver, 1980]. We hypothesize:

H1: (Dis)confirmation with a drug information supplier is determined by the degree and direction of the discrepancy between the physician's perceptions and expectations.

Woodside *et al.* [1989] and Bitner [1990] are some of the authors who showed that positive disconfirmation and confirmation influence satisfaction positively. As a construct satisfaction is a 'post-purchase' phenomenon reflecting how much the client likes or dislikes the service after experiencing it [Churchill and Surprenant, 1982]. In services marketing literature, confirmation or disconfirmation is also called 'perceived service quality' or 'PSQ' [Parasuraman, 1985]. Several authors have discussed the relationship between these two constructs. Does PSQ influence satisfaction or is it the other way round? Originally, PZB [1988] and Carman [1990] posited that an accumulation of satisfaction assessments leads to a global assessment of service quality. However, Cronin and Taylor [1992] provided empirical and literature support suggesting that PSQ (as an attitude) is an antecedent of satisfaction. Only recently, PZB (1994) revised their distinction, also suggesting to model service quality as an antecedent of customer satisfaction. Therefore, in our study we hypothesize:

H2: Satisfaction with a drug information supplier is determined by the level of (dis)confirmation which exists with respect to the drug information supplier.

Additionally, we hypothesize that if a physician is satisfied with a drug information source, he will use this source (again) as an advisor in a complex patient case. Therefore, a third hypothesis is that satisfaction shows a relationship with the importance attached to the information source in the decision-making process of a physician. This idea is also based on the relationship between satisfaction and behavioural intention found by Woodside *et al.* [1989] and Bitner [1990]. Based on these arguments we hypothesize:

H3: The importance attached to a drug information supplier depends positively on the level of satisfaction with this information supplier.

In other words, the larger the discrepancy between expectations and perceptions, the larger the negative disconfirmation, the less the satisfaction experienced by the physician, and the less the importance of the drug information supplier as perceived by the physician.

---

9   In consumer behaviour literature, the selection of an information source is mostly modelled as a cost-benefit analysis. Financial and behavioural costs are weighted against the expected benefits of making a better decision [Hawkins 1992]. Our approach, however, has been inspired by Wilton and Myers [1986], who distinguish four sub-processes of the construct 'information utilization': formation of utility expectations, the choice and use of information items, and the modification of utility judgements following (or during) actual information exposure.

Naturally, this process is influenced by the characteristics of the physician, and uncertainty, knowledge and experience affect his information search behaviour to a large extent. Sternthal and Craig [1982] state that individuals who are uncertain about a judgement task will look for more information than those who are less uncertain. The type of patient case and the importance of the case also play a role in this process. However, we do not include these variables in our model, because we assume that in the case of complex patient problems, the information provided by the drug information suppliers plays a dominant role. Therefore, the (therapy) choice made by a physician in a complex patient case is assumed to be a function of the importance attached to the information sources and the information received.

A point of interest concerns the measurement of expectations and perceptions, being the central concepts of our approach. A large number of authors have proposed dimensions which consumers use in forming expectations about and perceptions of services [Kotler, 1988; Zeithaml, Parasuraman and Berry, 1990]. Medical literature [Curley, Connely and Rich, 1989] can be used to 'translate' these dimensions into the specific dimensions which physicians use to evaluate drug information suppliers. In doing so, we have identified five dimensions which influence the expectations and perceptions of physicians: two technical (knowledge and interpretation) and three process dimensions (reliability, responsiveness and empathy). The precise meanings of the dimensions used in the context of this study are defined in Table 2.2.

Table 2.2   Definitions of the dimensions used in the present study

knowledge	the scope of knowledge and the degree of a close logical relationship to the problem under consideration; experience of the source
interpretation	the ease with which the provided information is understood and can be applied to the clinical situation
reliability	ability to perform the promised service dependably and accurately; reputation of the source
responsiveness	the speed and ease of access and availability of the source, and the speed and ease with which the information can be obtained from the source
empathy	politeness, respect and friendliness of the source

Figure 2.2 summarises the entire theoretical model based on the hypotheses. To test the hypotheses, empirical research was set up.

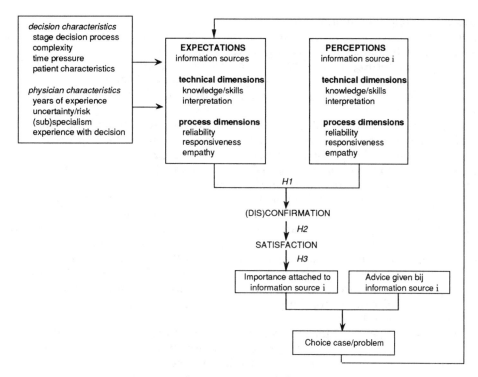

Figure 2.2 Decision-making process of hospital physicians in case of complex patient problems

Research Method

Measurement of the Variables Used in the Model

We chose internists to collect the data from, because they work in a drug-oriented manner and are relatively large in number (which is rather convenient for a quantitative study). A survey instrument was designed to capture the internists' perceptions and expectations of drug information sources. The starting point for each 19-page questionnaire was a complex patient case, related to the diagnosis, the therapy choice, or to the implementation stage of the therapy. These complex patient cases have been collected in a pilot study in which physicians were asked to formulate and evaluate complex patient problems out of their practice in which they consult personal information sources [Boerkamp *et al.*, 1993b]. We chose six cases, which were considered as complex problems by the physicians and referred to as cases involving several personal information sources. Two cases were related to diagnosis, two to therapy choice, and another two to implementation. The cases are presented in Appendix 1 (it is also indicated which stage a particular case belongs to). The information sources used in these cases have been categorised to allow for a structured quantitative analysis. The following four categories are distinguished (between brackets are the numbers of the cases in which the particular information source is applicable):

Source 1. Colleague internists (case 1-6);
Source 2. Sub-specialists: nephrologists (cases 1 and 5), cardiologists (cases 2 and 6), oncologist (case 3), surgeon (case 4);
Source 3. Supporting medical specialists: microbiologists (cases 1 and 4), NVIC (cases 2 and 5)[10], clinical pharmacologists (cases 3 and 6);
Source 4. Supporting non-medical professionals: hospital pharmacists (cases 1-6).

Because evaluation of six patient cases by one physician would be too time-consuming for the respondents, two partial questionnaires were developed: Q1 comprising questions related to patient cases 1 to 3, and Q2 containing questions related to cases 4 to 6. Within each partial questionnaire, the order of the three cases was varied to prevent order effects in the answers.

Each questionnaire was built up as follows: presentation of a patient case; questions about characteristics of the case (difficulty, risk of the decision, type of decision, and so forth); statements about expectations of a 'useful' information supplier for this case; statements about the perceptions of the four information sources appropriate in this case; a judgement about the (dis)confirmation, satisfaction, and importance of these four sources in this case. This battery of questions was repeated for all three cases. At the end of the questionnaire additional questions were asked concerning the physicians' background, including age, year of registration, type of hospital.

We refer to Appendix 2 for the precise phrasings of the expectation- and perception-related statements. (Dis)confirmation was measured on a 7-point Likert scale as 'Source 1 is a useful information source in this case' with 1 = very strongly disagree to 7 = very strongly agree. Satisfaction was operationalised as 'How satisfied are you with source i in this case?' (from 1 = extremely unsatisfied to 7 = extremely satisfied) and Importance as 'The chance of consulting source i for this case in reality' (from 1=very small to 7=very large).

Sampling and Data-Collection Procedure

A telephone-mail-telephone approach was chosen to collect the data. Out of a database of 892 Dutch internists, 601 internists were approached. Forty-four addresses were not useful for several reasons: retirement of the physician, relocation, or illness. Of the remaining 557 physicians, 496 agreed to fill in the questionnaire. As an inducement to participate in the study, physicians were offered a small financial reward or given the opportunity to donate this amount of money to charity ('Médecins sans Frontières'). After the telephone reminder, a total of 329 lists had been received, representing a net response rate of 59% (329/557). We received 172 Q1-type and 157 Q2-type of which 160 and 144, respectively, had been filled in correctly.

Internist respondents were classified into four registration-year categories; on average, 15% of them were registered before 1970, 36% between 1971-80, 39% between 1981-90, and 10% were registered after 1990. In conformity with the distribution in the sampling frame, about one third of the respondents worked in university hospitals and two-thirds in community hospitals. The geographical dispersion of the respondents was representative of the sampling frame with the exception of

---

10 NVIC is short for 'Nationaal Vergiftigingen Informatie Centrum', meaning the Dutch Poisoning and Information Centre.

the provinces of North-Holland and South-Holland (slightly underrepresented), and Groningen and Gelderland (slightly overrepresented). Most of the respondents (75%) spent more than 60 per cent of their time on patient care; 60% worked in a hospital with more than 600 beds (in conformity with the sampling frame).

Method of Analysis

The analysis of the data took place in three steps. First, the mean scores and standard deviations were computed, followed by assessment of the reliability of the explanatory variables. The differences between the perception and the expectation scores were computed for each physician. The items making up one dimension were added and divided by the number of items making up that dimension. Next, mean scores were computed. We used Cronbach's alpha and the recently proposed formula by Peter, Churchill and Brown [1993] to assess the internal consistency of the dimensions.

The third step was the explanation of the dependent variables (disconfirmation, satisfaction and importance, respectively). Multiple regression analysis was used to estimate the (dis)confirmation equation with the five dimensions as explanatory variables (H1). To estimate the satisfaction and importance equation simple regression was used with the estimated (dis)confirmation (H2) and the estimated satisfaction (H3), respectively, as explanatory variables. For all estimations in this stage, ordinary least squares regression was used, assuming normally distributed disturbance terms.

Results of the Empirical Research

Mean Scores of the Variables in the Model

Table 2.3 summarises the results of the mean scores and the standard deviations. Scores are given for the three dependent variables, (dis)confirmation, satisfaction and importance. The five quality dimensions that explain disconfirmation are also given. Because these scores are expressed as the difference between perceptions and expectations, a negative score means a shortcoming on that particular quality item of the information supplier in a patient case.

In case 1, a 'therapy choice' case, the colleague, nephrologist, and microbiologist appeared to be appropriate sources, as shown by the extremely small discrepancies between the perceptions and expectations on the five quality dimensions. The hospital pharmacist was perceived as less important. Especially with respect to the dimensions knowledge and reliability, the perceptions of his services did not meet the expectations of the internists. Detailed analyses of these answers indicated that the negative scores on knowledge and reliability for the hospital pharmacist were mainly due to his perceived lack of specialised knowledge and experience, as well as his bad reputation in this problem field, and to the fact that the information he provides about the problem is perceived to be inaccurate and clinically not applicable. Although the (dis)confirmation and satisfaction with the nephrologist was perceived as being high (5.97 and 6.06), the respondents indicated the microbiologist as the source which they would most likely consult about this case in reality (indicated by the importance scores).

Table 2.3   Mean scores and standard deviations of variables in the modified SERVQUAL model

	Case 1	Case 2	Case 3	Case 4	Case 5	Case 6
Source 1	*colleague int*					
(dis)confirmation	5.08 (1.54)	4.24 (1.68)	4.60 (1.90)	6.04 (1.23)	4.66 (1.64)	4.74 (1.74)
know$	-0.50 (1.35)	-1.04 (1.54)	-1.06 (1.56)	-0.10 (0.86)	-0.87 (1.41)	-0.61 (1.42)
inter	-0.16 (1.18)	-0.56 (1.25)	-0.48 (1.33)	0.00 (0.82)	-0.47 (1.19)	-0.20 (1.28)
reli	-0.78 (1.30)	-1.54 (1.33)	-1.29 (1.40)	-0.32 (0.99)	-1.43 (1.27)	-0.86 (1.33)
respo	-0.07 (1.19)	-0.89 (1.35)	-0.51 (1.22)	-0.10 (1.03)	-0.74 (1.26)	0.93 (1.50)
emp	0.58 (1.63)	0.55 (1.61)	0.74 (1.58)	0.67 (1.62)	0.71 (1.72)	0.58 (1.84)
satisfaction	5.34 (1.36)	4.84 (1.54)	4.96 (1.51)	5.99 (1.09)	4.96 (1.29)	5.32 (1.44)
importance	3.45 (1.99)	3.12 (1.87)	4.04 (2.12)	5.57 (1.74)	3.93 (2.07)	4.06 (2.14)
Source 2	*nephrologist*	*cardiologist*	*oncologist*	*surgeon*	*nephrologist*	*cardiologist*
(dis)confirmation	5.97 (1.21)	2.74 (1.68)	6.21 (1.11)	3.75 (1.95)	4.43 (1.81)	5.39 (1.55)
know	0.13 (1.04)	-2.82 (1.66)	0.01 (0.95)	-2.01 (1.73)	-0.94 (1.65)	-0.72 (1.31)
inter	0.14 (1.04)	-1.51 (1.64)	0.02 (0.95)	-1.09 (1.58)	-0.59 (1.34)	-0.24 (1.15)
reli	-0.16 (1.05)	-2.95 (1.44)	-0.19 (0.88)	-2.11 (1.63)	-1.44 (1.48)	-0.75 (1.36)
respo	0.08 (1.20)	-1.53 (1.56)	-0.24 (1.01)	-1.08 (1.58)	-0.87 (1.45)	0.83 (1.61)
emp	0.64 (1.59)	0.13 (1.91)	0.85 (1.43)	-0.02 (2.04)	0.58 (1.92)	0.40 (1.79)
satisfaction	6.06 (0.99)	3.33 (1.65)	6.14 (0.94)	4.55 (1.57)	4.96 (1.49)	5.50 (1.37)
importance	4.66 (2.07)	2.19 (1.70)	6.17 (1.32)	4.16 (2.20)	3.96 (2.15)	5.41 (2.04)
Source 3	*mic.biologist*	*NVIC*	*clin.pharm.*	*mic.biologist*	*NVIC*	*clin.pharm.*
(dis)confirmation	5.57 (1.33)	6.44 (1.01)	4.26 (1.84)	5.57 (1.37)	6.39 (1.10)	3.81 (1.87)
know	-0.68 (1.29)	0.20 (1.09)	-1.70 (1.42)	-0.99 (1.24)	0.12 (1.38)	-1.71 (1.51)
inter	-0.22 (1.00)	0.08 (0.99)	-1.27 (1.27)	-0.58 (1.04)	-0.19 (1.17)	-1.22 (1.43)
reli	-0.59 (1.13)	-0.02 (0.90)	-1.72 (1.49)	-0.68 (1.31)	-0.10 (1.14)	-1.62 (1.56)
respo	0.05 (1.28)	0.42 (0.89)	-1.74 (1.59)	-0.57 (1.22)	0.30 (1.02)	-0.44 (1.56)
emp	0.68 (1.54)	0.69 (1.49)	0.34 (1.78)	0.52 (1.69)	0.83 (1.79)	0.11 (1.81)
satisfaction	5.69 (1.16)	6.11 (1.05)	4.33 (1.44)	5.62 (1.19)	6.12 (1.16)	4.43 (1.81)
importance	5.16 (1.73)	6.27 (1.29)	2.91 (1.81)	5.66 (1.63)	5.77 (1.88)	2.70 (1.83)
Source 4	*hosp.pharm.*					
(dis)confirmation	2.86 (1.54)	5.46 (1.43)	3.75 (1.80)	2.61 (1.57)	5.10 (1.65)	2.89 (1.71)
know	-2.59 (1.63)	-0.85 (1.57)	-2.09 (1.53)	-3.07 (1.48)	-1.15 (1.64)	-2.30 (1.47)
inter	-1.38 (1.35)	-0.50 (1.29)	-1.25 (1.44)	-1.80 (1.49)	-0.74 (1.41)	-1.36 (1.52)
reli	-2.11 (1.51)	-0.83 (1.30)	-1.84 (1.47)	-2.53 (1.51)	-1.06 (1.42)	-1.90 (1.49)
respo	0.74 (1.55)	-0.60 (1.27)	-0.85 (1.38)	-1.36 (1.51)	-0.83 (1.39)	0.28 (1.82)
emp	0.45 (1.77)	0.56 (1.61)	0.58 (1.76)	0.23 (2.05)	0.67 (1.91)	0.33 (1.93)
satisfaction	3.95 (1.53)	5.44 (1.42)	4.44 (1.49)	3.87 (1.61)	5.17 (1.45)	4.13 (1.50)
importance	2.36 (1.69)	5.01 (1.97)	3.24 (2.07)	2.31 (1.65)	4.51 (2.09)	2.45 (1.77)

&   mean scores are given; standard deviations between brackets; scores are based on a 7-point Likert scale.

$ know=knowledge, inter=interpretation, reli=reliability, respo=responsiveness, emp=empathy.

For case 2, a 'diagnosis' case, the NVIC and hospital pharmacist scores were high, indicating that they were considered as useful information sources in this case. The NVIC had no shortcomings on any quality aspect. In particular its reputation and experience in this field were perceived as good. The slightly lower score for the hospital pharmacist was caused by the fact that he was perceived to have less specialized knowledge than the NVIC in this field (-1.24 and 0.08, respectively). The colleague internist and in particular the specialized colleague, the cardiologist, fall short with respect to knowledge and reliability.

The oncologist was mentioned as the most suitable information source for 'implementation' case 3; the respondents also indicated that consulting him in reality for this problem was very probable. The clinical pharmacologist and the hospital pharmacist were considered less appropriate in general. For both professions this was mainly due to their lack of experience and knowledge in this field, and their modest reputation.

Similar to 'therapy choice' case 1, the hospital pharmacist is the source which the respondent were least satisfied with in case 4. The main reason for this is his lack of knowledge in this field.

The 'diagnosis' case 5 showed the same pattern as case 2. Both cases were concerned with intoxication problems and, as expected, the NVIC was perceived as the most suitable information supplier with a high chance of being consulted in reality. Again, the hospital pharmacist was the second-best possibility according to the respondents. This time the lower scores for the colleague and the nephrologist can be explained mainly by low scores on reliability aspects: accuracy of the information provided and reputation of the information supplier.

In case 6, the cardiologist was perceived as most appropriate. In fact, the same pattern as in case 3 can be observed, although even the best information source had shortcomings on the knowledge aspects.

Reliability of the Explanatory Variables

Since the five dimensions explaining (dis)confirmation were constructed *a priori*, it was necessary to test their reliability. Traditionally, in the services marketing literature, internal consistency reliability is assessed using Cronbach's [1951] coefficient alpha. Table 2.4 shows the computed alphas of the internists' sample. Each column gives the *a*-scores for a particular information source belonging to a patient case. As there were six patient cases and four sources per case, the alphas are given for 24 situations. A score above 0.7 is interpreted as reliable, a score between 0.5 and 0.7 as acceptable, and a score below 0.5 as weak [Nunnaly, 1967]. We can conclude that the dimensions knowledge (KNOW), reliability (RELI), and responsiveness (RESPO) are acceptable and in most cases reliable. The internal consistencies of the dimension interpretation (INTER) are rather low. The alphas suggested that the dimensions are reasonably reliable, but also that the results of the analyses to follow should be approached with caution in case of the dimension interpretation.

Described above is the classical reliability theory. However, Peter *et al.* [1993] have recently cautioned for using difference scores in consumer research, for a variety of reasons. They argue that using Cronbach's coefficient alpha to assess reliability of a difference score is inappropriate, because it does not adequately consider the correlation between the perception and expectation components of the quality dimensions. They suggest a formula that does consider the correlation between P and E scores. Table 2.4 also shows the reliability scores based on this formula. The results did not diverge much from the Cronbach's alpha. Only for the NVIC in case 2 and the oncologist in case 3 the r_D-scores on the dimension knowledge performed worse. The conclusion mentioned above that the dimension interpretation has to be interpreted with care in our regression analysis in view of the moderate alpha-values is even more justified when looking at the r_D-scores.

Table 2.4 *Internal consistencies of the five dimensions of service (dis)confirmation with four information sources*[$]

dim/no. items[*]			Case 1				Case 2				Case 3			
			col#[#]	nep	mic	hp	col	car	nvic	hp	col	onc	cp	hp
KNOW	3	α	.669	.678	.704	.741	.617	.733	.580	.744	.664	.543	.720	.762
		r_D	.691	.501	.617	.742	.659	.719	.274	.690	.692	.262	.675	.724
INTER	2	α	.575	.667	.493	.363	.489	.509	.554	.671	.624	.598	.464	.591
		r_D	.497	.527	.360	.489	.465	.493	.399	.586	.550	.447	.413	.529
RELI	3	α	.780	.729	.754	.744	.708	.670	.642	.766	.745	.699	.769	.750
		r_D	.755	.671	.668	.719	.691	.644	.610	.747	.732	.620	.778	.727
RESPO	3	α	.740	.778	.831	.805	.774	.784	.780	.791	.764	.742	.865	.778
		r_D	.723	.743	.789	.779	.768	.761	.725	.801	.754	.692	.856	.796
EMP[%]	1													

dim/no. items[*]			Case 4				Case 5				Case 6			
			col#[#]	surg	mic	hp	col	nep	nvic	hp	col	car	cp	hp
KNOW	3	α	.557	.824	.694	.701	.610	.742	.659	.786	.631	.745	.661	.638
		r_D	.415	.816	.620	.713	.596	.711	.579	.720	.607	.597	.658	.631
INTER	2	α	.392	.552	.396	.448	.513	.648	.654	.652	.540	.553	.583	.592
		r_D	.220	.498	.233	.409	.399	.558	.574	.633	.491	.557	.528	.505
RELI	3	α	.718	.770	.788	.714	.711	.767	.817	.727	.713	.751	.712	.690
		r_D	.699	.754	.783	.709	.696	.767	.787	.767	.654	.700	.657	.641
RESPO	3	α	.831	.855	.812	.789	.817	.862	.815	.854	.750	.803	.772	.805
		r_D	.781	.844	.781	.768	.799	.852	.798	.847	.704	.755	.702	.769
EMP[%]	1													

[$]   The upper score in each cell represents Cronbach's alpha, the lower score is the reliability score, corrected for correlation between the components.

[*]   dim./ no.items = the first column shows the dimensions; the second column the number of items in the scale.

[#]   Abbreviations used in this table represent the following information sources: col=colleague, nep=nephrologist, mic=microbiologist, hp=hospital pharmacist, car=cardiologist, nvic=nationaal vergiftigingen informatiecentrum, onc=oncologist, cp= clinical pharmacologist, surg=surgeon.

[%]   Internal consistencies cannot be computed (dimension consists of one item).

Estimation of the Parameters

Results for (dis)confirmation, satisfaction and importance are presented in Tables 2.5 and 2.6.

Disconfirmation. The relationship between (dis)confirmation and the five distinguished dimensions was significant (F-ratios varied from 3.71 to 40.24) for each drug information supplier distinguished in a particular patient case. On average two variables made statistically significant ($p<0.05$) contributions to the model.

Both a technical dimension (knowledge) and a process dimension (reliability) were significant predictors, each in the expected positive direction. In 18 of the 24 situations distinguished, the variable 'reliability' contributed more to (dis)confirmation with an information supplier than 'knowledge'. The dimensions empathy and responsiveness were in three and two cases significant, respectively. These dimensions did, however, have an unexpected negative sign. In case 4, 'interpretation' made a significant contribution to the explanation of (dis)confirmation with the microbiologist.

Table 2.5   *Parameter estimates of the (dis)confirmation equation, ols.*

		inter-cept	know$	inter	reli	respo	emp	R^2	adj.R^2	n
CASE 1										
source 1	colleague	5.61*	0.28*	-0.11	0.53*	-0.06	0.02	0.34	0.32	150
source 2	nephrologist	6.05*	0.05	-0.04	0.40*	-0.02	-0.02	0.12	0.09	146
source 3	microbiologist	5.99*	0.48*	-0.11	0.22	-0.10	0.03	0.29	0.26	147
source 4	hosp pharmacist	4.10*	0.15	0.12	0.34*	-0.06	-0.02	0.26	0.24	149
CASE 2										
source 1	colleague	5.46*	0.27*	0.01	0.50*	0.11	-0.12	0.40	0.38	148
source 2	cardiologist	5.09*	0.23*	0.01	0.59*	-0.04	-0.03	0.43	0.41	144
source 3	nvic	6.60*	0.21*	0.11	0.53*	-0.25*	-0.12*	0.33	0.30	151
source 4	hosp pharmacist	6.06*	0.35*	0.16	0.21o	0.09	-0.02	0.49	0.47	151
CASE 3										
source 1	colleague	5.79*	0.12	0.03	0.69*	0.08	-0.16o	0.36	0.34	140
source 2	oncologist	6.30*	0.20	-0.12	0.39*	0.05	-0.02	0.15	0.12	141
source 3	clin pharm	5.65*	0.40*	0.09	0.49*	-0.15	-0.07	0.37	0.35	125
source 4	hosp pharmacist	5.68*	0.39*	-0.04	0.70*	-0.19o	-0.06	0.55	0.53	142
CASE 4										
source 1	colleague	6.28*	0.28*	0.11	0.59*	-0.66	-0.04	0.39	0.38	140
source 2	surgeon	5.70*	0.54*	0.22o	0.30*	-0.01	-0.17*	0.60	0.58	141
source 3	microbiologist	6.29*	0.20*	0.43*	0.45*	-0.17o	-0.10o	0.52	0.50	140
source 4	hosp pharmacist	5.03*	0.55*	0.20o	0.19o	-0.10	-0.07	0.53	0.51	140
CASE 5										
source 1	colleague	5.91*	0.26*	0.34	0.70*	-0.05	-0.08	0.49	0.47	138
source 2	nephrologist	5.67*	0.29*	0.11	0.69*	-0.17	-0.11	0.51	0.49	138
source 3	nvic	6.55*	0.14	0.09	0.45*	-0.18o	-0.08	0.30	0.27	140
source 4	hosp pharmacist	6.20*	0.17o	0.05	0.66*	0.12	-0.12*	0.60	0.58	138
CASE 6										
source 1	colleague	5.56*	0.74*	-0.14	0.26*	-0.13	-0.09	0.43	0.41	136
source 2	cardiologist	6.13*	0.58*	0.01	0.39*	0.01	-0.11o	0.59	0.57	136
source 3	clin pharm	5.53*	0.42*	0.03	0.63*	-0.14	-0.03	0.58	0.56	115
source 4	hosp pharmacist	4.82*	0.24*	0.01	0.68*	-0.16*	-0.09	0.42	0.40	132

$ know=knowledge, inter=interpretation, reli=reliability, respo=responsiveness, emp=empathy
*   significance level 95%
o   significance level 90%

Satisfaction with the drug information source. As expected, the estimated (dis)confirmation (i.e., the part of disconfirmation that is explained by the five quality dimensions) contributed significantly to the explanation of satisfaction. We can conclude that H2 is confirmed: satisfaction with a drug information source is determined by the level of (dis)confirmation which exists between perceptions and expectations of the drug information supplier.

Importance attached to the drug information source. In the final equation, the estimated satisfaction made a significant ($p < 0.05$) contribution to the equation, which explains the importance attached to an information source. This confirms H3: the importance attached to a drug information source depends positively on the level of satisfaction with this information source.

Table 2.6   Parameter estimates of the satisfaction/importance equations, ols.

		SATISFACTION EQUATION				IMPORTANCE EQUATION			
		inter-cept	conf.&	R^2	adj.R^2	inter-cept	sat.$	R^2	adj.R^2
CASE 1									
source 1	colleague	0.50	0.95*	0.39	0.39	-0.95	0.82*	0.12	0.12
source 2	nephrologist	-0.71	1.13*	0.22	0.22	-1.56	1.03*	0.05	0.05
source 3	microbiologist	1.09	0.83*	0.25	0.25	-2.00	1.26*	0.18	0.18
source 4	hosp pharmacist	1.01*	1.03*	0.28	0.28	-1.77*	1.05*	0.25	0.25
CASE 2									
source 1	colleague	0.79*	0.95*	0.44	0.43	-1.38*	0.93*	0.25	0.25
source 2	cardiologist	0.92*	0.88*	0.35	0.35	-1.00*	0.96*	0.30	0.29
source 3	nvic	0.84	0.82*	0.20	0.20	1.28	0.82*	0.09	0.08
source 4	hosp pharmacist	-0.14	1.02*	0.52	0.52	-2.44	1.37*	0.50	0.50
CASE 3									
source 1	colleague	0.74o	0.92*	0.48	0.47	-2.02*	1.22*	0.36	0.36
source 2	oncologist	0.59	0.90*	0.17	0.17	1.10	0.83*	0.06	0.05
source 3	clin pharm	0.72o	0.85*	0.44	0.44	-1.44*	1.01*	0.28	0.27
source 4	hosp pharmacist	1.66*	0.74*	0.44	0.44	-2.43*	1.28*	0.37	0.37
CASE 4									
source 1	colleague	0.51	0.91*	0.41	0.41	-1.61	1.20*	0.23	0.23
source 2	surgeon	2.32*	0.59*	0.33	0.33	-3.05*	1.58*	0.42	0.41
source 3	microbiologist	0.91*	0.85*	0.49	0.49	-1.24o	1.23*	0.40	0.39
source 4	hosp pharmacist	2.10*	0.68*	0.23	0.23	-3.17*	1.42*	0.44	0.44
CASE 5									
source 1	colleague	1.28*	0.79*	0.51	0.50	-1.11	1.01*	0.20	0.19
source 2	nephrologist	1.39*	0.81*	0.50	0.50	-1.80*	1.16*	0.32	0.32
source 3	nvic	-1.18	1.14*	0.33	0.33	-2.13o	1.29*	0.22	0.22
source 4	hosp pharmacist	1.13*	0.79*	0.48	0.48	-2.58*	1.37*	0.44	0.43
CASE 6									
source 1	colleague	1.22*	0.87*	0.48	0.47	-1.61o	1.06*	0.24	0.24
source 2	cardiologist	1.09*	0.82*	0.51	0.51	-1.21	1.20*	0.33	0.32
source 3	clin pharm	1.92*	0.66*	0.42	0.42	-1.81*	1.02*	0.27	0.27
source 4	hosp pharmacist	2.02*	0.73*	0.29	0.29	-2.61*	1.23*	0.31	0.31

&	conf=the estimated (dis)confirmation
$	sat=the estimated satisfaction
*	significance level 95%
o	significance level 90%

Conclusions

In this chapter, we presented a research model to assess the impact of service quality provided by drug information suppliers on the behaviour of the physician, the professional customer. Therefore, a sample of Dutch internists evaluated four different categories of drug information sources in terms of expectations and perceptions of their service quality in six complex patient cases.

The most important hypothesis (H1) 'the (dis)confirmation with a drug information source can be explained by the difference between perceptions and expectations' received strong support. On average two dimensions made a significant contribution, both a technical (knowledge) and a process dimension (reliability). It appeared that concerning knowledge, it was a matter of (perceived) lack of specialised knowledge of and experience with a particular information source. With respect to reliability, the preciseness of the information and the reputation of the information source were perceived as important aspects. Furthermore, the results showed that the level of (dis)confirmation determined the level of satisfaction with a drug information source (H2) and the level of satisfaction determined positively the importance attached to an information source (H3).

Concerning relationships between professional health care providers (the information suppliers) and customers (the physicians), both a technical dimension and a process dimension are important to explain (dis)confirmation. This finding is not congruent with the results from consumer service quality research, in which process dimensions appeared to be decisive for judgements about service quality. For example, Reidenbach and Sandifer-Smallwood [1990] found that for patient-evaluating hospital services, 'patient confidence' was the dominant dimension. The results, however, are more in line with the scarce studies on relationships between professionals, in which it is concluded that expertise plays an important role when a professional customer evaluates service quality [Day and Barksdale, 1992].

The findings must be interpreted in light of the limitations inherent in the study method. Although the results show that the constructs used provided positive evidence of reliability and validity, the external validity is questionable. The target group for the empirical study were internists. Variability in the use of information source across specialities, however, cannot be determined with confidence. Also, the exclusion of written and computer-based drug information sources may inflate the importance of personal drug information sources.

The three hypotheses investigated here are offered as an initial step toward better understanding the relationships between professionals in hospitals. In future analyses we will elaborate on the results presented in this chapter. We will investigate as to whether it is possible to generalise our findings by aggregating over information sources and over patient cases. However, we might also investigate the results on a more disaggregated level and see whether there are possibilities for segmentation. Differences may be found between community and university hospitals, or between small and large hospitals.

References

Bering, R., 1992, 'Kwaliteitsbeleid - Wat er van Leidschendam terechtkwam', *Medisch Contact*, 47, Nr.8 (February), pp.241-244.

Bitner, M.J., 1990, 'Evaluating Service Encounters: The Effects of Physical Surroundings and Employee Responses', *Journal of Marketing*, 54, pp.69-82.

Boerkamp, E.J.C., Haaijer-Ruskamp, F.M., Reuyl, J.C. and A. Versluis, 1993a, 'Impact of Service Quality on Behaviour of Professional Customers: Selection and Use of Drug Information Suppliers by Physicians', In: Proceedings 3rd Workshop on Quality Management in Services, EIASM, Helsinki, pp.37-52.

Boerkamp, E.J.C., Haaijer-Ruskamp, F.M., Reuyl, J.C. and A. Versluis, 1993b, 'The Use of Drug Information Sources by Physicians: Development of a Data-Generating Methodology', internal research paper.

Boerkamp, E.J.C., Versluis, A., Reuyl, J.C., Haaijer-Ruskamp, F.M., Witsen, T. van and R. de Wolf, 1992, 'The Changing Role of the Hospital-based Pharmacist: A Comparative Study of the Dutch and the English Situation', In: Proceedings 2nd Workshop on Strategies for the Pharmaceutical Industries, EIASM, Brussels, September 7-8.

Carman, J.M., 1990, 'Consumer Perceptions of Service Quality: An Assessment of the SERVQUAL Dimensions', *Journal of Retailing*, 66 (1), pp.33-55.

Churchill Jr, G.A. and C. Surprenant, 'An Investigation into the Determinants of Customer Satisfaction', *Journal of Marketing Research*, 19, November, 1982, pp.491-504.

Cronbach, L., 1951, 'Coefficient Alpha and the Internal Structure of Tests', *Psychometrika*, 14, pp.297-334.

Cronin, J.J. and S.A. Taylor, 1992, 'Measuring Service Quality: A Reexamination and Extension', *Journal of Marketing*, 56, pp.55-68.

Curley, S.P., Connely, D. and E.C. Rich, 1989, 'Physicians' Use of Medical Knowledge Resources: Preliminary Theoretical Framework and Findings', *Medical Decision Making*, 10, pp.231-241.

Day, E. and H.C. Barksdale, 1992, 'How Firms Select Professional Services', *Industrial Marketing Management*, 21, pp.85-91.

Denig, P. and F.M. Haaijer-Ruskamp, 1992, 'Therapeutic Decision Making of Physicians', *Pharmaceutisch Weekblad Scientific Edition*, 14 (1), pp.9-15.

Gardner, 1986, Dissertation Proposal, Washington: George Washington University.

Grönroos, C., 1984, 'A Service Quality Model and Its Marketing Implications', *European Journal of Marketing*, 18 (4), pp.36-44.

Grönroos, C., 1990, *Service Management and Marketing: Managing the Moments of Truth in Service Competition*, Massachusetts/Toronto: Lexington Books.

Hawkins, D.I., Best, R.J. and K.A. Coney, 1992, *Consumer Behavior: Implications for Marketing Strategy*, Homewood/Boston: Irwin.

Hitchings, C., 1989, 'The Pharmacist and Information Flow to the Hospital Physician', in I. Lunde and G. Dukes (eds.), *The Role and Function of the Pharmacist in Europe*, Groningen: Styx Publications.

Kotler, P., 1988, *Marketing Management: Analysis, Planning, Implementation, and Control*, Englewood Cliffs, NJ: Prentice Hall.

Lovelock, C.H., 1991, *Services Marketing*, Englewood Cliffs, NJ: Prentice Hall.

Nunnaly, J.C., 1967, *Psychometric Theory*, New York: Mc-Graw Hill Book Company.

Oliver, R.L., 1980, 'A Cognitive Model of the Antecedents and Consequence of Satisfaction Decisions', *Journal of Marketing Research*, 17, pp.460-469.

Ortiz, M., Walker, W.L. and R. Thomas, 1989, 'Physicians - Friend or Foe? Comparison between Pharmacists' and Physicians' Perceptions of the Pharmacists Role', *Journal of Social and Administrative Pharmacy*, 6 (2), pp.59-68.

Parasuraman, A., Zeithaml, V.A. and L.L. Berry, 1985, 'A Conceptual Model of Service Quality and its Implications for Future Research', *Journal of Marketing*, 49, pp.41-50.

Parasuraman, A., Zeithaml, V.A. and L.L. Berry, 1988, 'SERVQUAL: A Multiple-Item Scale for Measuring Consumer Perceptions of Service Quality', *Journal of Retailing*, 64 (Spring), pp.12-40.

Parasuraman, A., Zeithaml, V.A. and L.L. Berry, 1994, 'Reassessment of Expectations as a Comparison Standard in Measuring Service Quality: Implications for Further Research', *Journal of Marketing*, 58 (January), pp.111-124.

Peter, J.P., Churchill G.A., and T.J. Brown, 1993, 'Caution in the Use of Difference Scores in Consumer Research', *Journal of Consumer Research*, 19, pp.655-662.

Peyrot, M., Cooper, P.D. and D. Schnapf, 1993, 'Consumer Satisfaction and Perceived Service Quality of Outpatient Health Services', *Journal of Health Care Marketing*, Winter, pp.24-33.

Reidenbach, R.E. and B. Sandifer-Smallwood, 1990, 'Exploring Perceptions of Hospital Operations by a Modified SERVQUAL Approach', *Journal of Health Care Marketing*, 10 (4), pp.47-55.

Sternthal, B. and S.S. Craig, 1982, *Consumer Behavior: An Information Processing Perspective*, Englewood Cliffs, NJ: Prentice Hall.

Williams, J.R. and P.J. Hensel, 1991, 'Changes in Physicians' Sources of Pharmaceutical Information: A Review', *Journal of Health Care Marketing*, 11, pp.46-60.

Wilton, P.C. and J.G. Myers, 1986, 'Task, Expectancy, and Information Assessment Effects in Information Utilization Processes', *Journal of Consumer Research*, 12, pp.469-486.

Woodside, A.G., Frey L.L. and R.T. Daly, 1989, 'Linking Service Quality, Customer Satisfaction, and Behavioral Intention', *Journal of Health Care Marketing*, 9, pp.5-17.

Zeithaml, V.A., Parasuraman, A. and L.L. Berry, 1990, *Delivering Quality Service: Balancing Customer Perceptions and Expectations*, New York: The Free Press.

APPENDIX 1: Cases in the Questionnaires

Questionnaire 1
1. THERAPY CHOICE
A woman, aged 69, is admitted to the hospital with a high fever. She had a history of corralites with a relapsing urinary tract infection. The laboratory results show a 'dirty' sediment, the number of leucocytes is 14.7, and the differential is 23 bars. The renal function has worsened in recent years, the serum creatinine concentration is 670 µmol/l. What is your (treatment) policy?

2. DIAGNOSIS
A woman, aged 59, with a psychiatric background is admitted to the hospital in a comatose state. According to her relatives she took all of her prescribed medications at one time. Empty boxes of lithium carbonate, amitryptiline and two benzodiapines were found. Do you administer Anexate (flumazenil) to this patient?

3. IMPLEMENTATION
A woman, aged 28, is treated on an in-patient basis for metastatic carcinoma of the chorion. The cytostatics used include methotrexate (1.0 g/m2). Supportive therapy consists of hyperhydration and sodium bicarbonate. Despite these supportive measures she develops oliguria during the MTX infusion. What actions are to be taken?

Questionnaire 2
4. THERAPY CHOICE
A woman, aged 72, is referred to hospital by a general practitioner because of high fever and confusion. She has not yet been treated with antibiotics. At the moment of admittance to the hospital she is confused, hypotensive (RR 80/40), with a heart rate of 140/min. and a temperature of 41 °C. Her right upper arm is swollen, red and infiltrated to the arm pit. The arteria radialis and ulnaris right are hardly palpable. There is a small injury on the elbow. The skin of the entire body shows a light rash. Upon observation an anuria is seen. After venal puncture there is continued bleeding. The laboratory results show a thrombocyte count of $13.10^9/l$, a serum potassium of 6.9 µmol/l, urea of 30 µmol/l, creatinine of 270 µmol/l, SGOT of 2000, and SGPT of 3500. You suspect a toxic syndrome with severe rhabdomyolysis. Which treatments do you think are necessary?

5. DIAGNOSIS
A man, aged 45, is referred to the hospital for an attempted suicide by ingestion of a large amount of methylated spirit some hours earlier. On the time of arrival the man is comatose. The blood is not very acidotic and the methanol concentration is presently below 500 milligram per litre. What is your policy?

6. IMPLEMENTATION
A woman, aged 32, with a prosthetic mitral valve wants to become pregnant. She uses phenprocumon as an anticoagulant and oral contraceptives. What do you advise?

APPENDIX 2: Independent Variables

The independent variables which explain (dis)confirmation consisted of five dimensions: knowledge, interpretation, reliability, responsiveness, empathy. Each dimension consisted of a number of statements and has been measured as the difference between perceptions and expectations with respect to these statements (see below). In the questionnaires the statements were measured on a 7-point Likert scale ranging from 'very strongly disagree' (=1) to 'very strongly agree' (=7).

The expectation statements can be derived from the phrasings below by filling in 'a useful information supplier' instead of '...'. To derive the perception statements the appropriate information supplier for a particular patient case has to be filled in here. For example, in patient case 1, one of the information sources distinguished is the colleague internist. The perception statements for the colleague can be obtained by filling in 'my colleague' instead of '...'. We refer to section 3 for an overview of the information sources used in a particular case. We developed the following 13 statements related to the five dimensions.

Knowledge (KNOW)
° ... possesses specialized knowledge related to this patient case.
° ... possesses extensive, broad knowledge.
° ... is experienced in solving this patient case.

Interpretation (INTER)
° ... gives an answer which is clinically applicable.
° ... provides information which is easy to understand.

Reliability (RELI)
° ... has a good reputation in the field related to this patient case.
° ... provides accurate information.
° ... provides the information at the time promised.

Responsiveness (RESPO)
° ... provides a prompt answer.
° ... can be easily reached.
° ... is accessible by telephone.
° ... is directly available to solve this problem.

Empathy (EMP)
° ... approaches me in a friendly manner.

3

Financial Advice: Observing the Client-Advisor Interaction Process

Harriëtte Greve, Ruud Frambach and Theo Verhallen[1]

This study explores the advice interaction in a mortgage setting. A total of 46 conversations within 26 interactions between advisors and clients have been observed. The exact contents and type of the interactions have been tape-recorded. The complete interactions have been coded using Bales' interaction category system and a coding system based on consultative selling. Both coding systems are based on a problem-solving sequence of the advice interaction process. The results indicate large differences between advisors in their client approach. The results show that the sequence of problem-solving phases often differs from the ideal model. Often the advisor did not probe for client wishes but started with a presentation of alternative product solutions, which is typical of a hard selling approach. Direct observation seems to be a revealing method for studying the advisory process.

Introduction

The personal interaction between an organisation and its customers is a valuable topic for research in marketing [Webster, 1968]. Within the stream of literature applying the dyadic interaction view [Evans, 1963; Johnston and Bonoma, 1984; Iacobucci and Hopkins, 1992], an abundant number of studies have been conducted in order to explain personal selling behaviour [Pennington, 1968; Bagozzi, 1978; Weitz, 1981]. Most of the studies that examined the face-to-face selling interaction considered durable consumer goods [Willett and Pennington, 1966; Olhavsky, 1973; Capon, 1975] and industrial goods [Pennington, 1968; Spiro and Perreault, 1979]. However, in the service industry the personal interaction is even of more importance than in other industries [Solomon, Surprenant, Czepiel and Gutman, 1985]. Service marketers increasingly recognise the need to better understand the

---

1   University of Tilburg, P.O. Box 90153, 5000 LE Tilburg, The Netherlands

interactive process in the service encounter in order to achieve more successful results.

In personal selling research, the existing body of knowledge has focused on the relationship between effectiveness, selling behaviour and a variety of seller and buyer characteristics [Weitz, 1981]. Previous conceptualisations of the buyer-seller interaction suggest a number of variables and relationships between these variables which are important to the understanding of the interaction [Williams, Spiro and Fine 1990]. As stated by Williams *et al.* (1990), most of these studies have been very limited in their scope, largely ignoring the interactive nature of two-way communication between the buyer and seller [Farley and Swinth, 1967; Evans, 1963; Weitz, 1978]. Several empirical studies include elements of the interpersonal communication process [Chapple and Gordon, 1947; Willett and Pennington, 1966; Pennington, 1968; Hulbert and Capon, 1972; Olhavsky, 1973; Soldow and Thomas, 1984; Williams and Spiro, 1985]. In a recent discussion of the interactive aspects of personal selling by Williams *et al.* (1990), the growing need to focus future research efforts on the actual buyer/seller interaction is highlighted. Instead of using surveys of buyers or sellers and laboratory investigations, they stress the need for observation methodologies, such as the analysis of sales interactions by Willett and Pennington (1966).

The goal of the present study is to explore the actual client-advisor behaviour in a mortgage setting using observation. As stated by Stafford [1992], an advantage of observation is that it ensures an integral and accurate description of the complete client-advisor interaction. The way advisors say they behave in an interaction may differ from their actual behaviour. In theory, the mortgage advice interaction can be viewed as a task-oriented process in which the advisor tries to find a solution for the individual needs (or problem) of the client. In the literature, the problem-solving approach is frequently used [Engel, Blackwell and Kollat, 1978]. The emphasis in problem solving is, first, on identifying the client's problem by gaining information from the buyer about his or her needs and preferences. Second, once the buyer's requirements and circumstances are fully understood, the seller can accommodate the product offering to the buyer's needs [Campbell, Graham, Jolibert and Meissner, 1988]. We assume that the problem-solving approach is applied in the mortgage advice interaction.

In this study we investigate whether the problem-solving process actually takes place in the practice of mortgage advice. The analysis is based on two coding systems. First, we adopted the interaction system originally defined by Bales [1950] to study social behaviour in small group interactions. Bales' coding method is praised in the literature for its objectivity and conceptual structure [Rogers and Farace, 1975]. However, the theoretical categories in Bales' system poses difficulties in the empirical implementation of the problem-solving sequence. A more pragmatic problem-solving method is recognised in the literature as the consultative selling model [Chevalier, 1993; Smith, 1991; Keenan, 1993]. In the consultative selling method the emphasis is on determining the specific needs of the client. Based on a clear identification of these needs, suggestions or solutions are presented [Picarelli, 1989]. The consultative selling model as defined by Picarelli [1989] was adopted as the second coding system in order to capture the problem-solving phases in mortgage advice interactions.

First, the Bales system and the consultative selling model will be explained. Then, we will describe the empirical study and report the results. Finally, the findings will be discussed and future implications will be given.

Theory

Bales

From the number of category schemes concerned with describing interactive communication processes, the coding scheme of Bales has been one of the systems most frequently used in personal selling contexts [Angelmar and Stern, 1978]. Although Bales' method is criticised for its deficiency of communication categories that include instrumental behaviour like promises and threats [McGrath and Julian, 1963], it is praised in the literature for its accurate use in those selling contexts in which social interaction theoretically can be viewed as a form of problem solving, more than as a form of conflict resolution [Angelmar and Stern, 1978]. Bales' coding system for interactive behaviour consists of twelve categories that are used to classify dyadic behaviour on an act-by-act basis (Table 3.1).

Table 3.1 Bales' categories

DEFINITION OF INTERACTION CATEGORIES

Social-Emotional Area: Positive Rewards	1. *Shows solidarity*, raises other's status, gives help, reward (f) 2. *Shows tension release*, jokes, laughs, shows satisfaction (e) 3. *Agrees*, shows passive acceptance, understands, complies (d)
Task-Area: Attempted Answers	4. *Gives suggestion*, direction, implying autonomy for other (c) 5. *Gives opinion*, evaluation, analysis, expresses feeling, wish (b) 6. *Gives orientation*, information, repeats, clarifies, confirms (a)
Task-Area: Questions	7. *Asks for orientation*, information, repeats, clarifies, confirms (a) 8. *Asks for opinion*, evaluation, analysis, expresion of feeling (b) 9. *Asks for suggestion*, direction, possible ways of action (c)
Social-Emotional Area: Negative Reactions	10. *Disagrees*, shows passive rejection, withholds help (d) 11. *Shows tension*, asks for help, withdraws out of field (e) 12. *Shows antagonism*, deflates other's status, defends (f)

a. Problems of orientation	d. Problems of decision
b. Problems of evaluation	e. Problems of tension-management
c. Problems of control	f. Problems of integration

Source: Robert F. Bales, 'A Set of Categories for the Analysis of Small Group Interaction', *American Sociological Review*, April, 1950, p.258.

The observational categories refer to task-oriented problems on the one hand and socio-emotional-oriented problems on the other. The task-oriented problems are dealt with primarily by the expression of attempted answers and questions. The socio-emotional problems are handled basically by the expression of positive and negative reactions [Bales, 1950; Rogers and Farace, 1975; Angelmar and Stern, 1978].

According to Bales theory, dyadic interactions include six problem-solving phases, i.e., problems of orientation, problems of evaluation, problems of control, problems of decision, problems of tension-management and problems of integration (1950). Bales' phases are frequently used in buyer-seller studies to evaluate the type of communication in interaction processes. Yet, the related sequence of these phases in problem-solving continue to be vague.

Consultative Selling

According to Picarelli (1989) the consultative selling approach covers four problem-solving phases. These phases are sequentially:

1) establish rapport and confirm objectives;
2) probe for information and listen for/determine clients' needs;
3) present programme;
4) resolve objections, close the sale or establish next steps.

In the consultative selling approach the consultant is required to help clients to improve their profits, instead of persuading them to purchase products and services [Hanan, 1988]. Products with a high degree of complexity that require a match between product features and customer needs, will best fit the consultative selling process [Chevalier, 1993]. Therefore, the consultative selling approach should be useful for both the advisor and the client in the mortgage advice interaction.

Granger (1988), Hubbard (1988) and Creeth (1989) also distinguished sub-phases in consultative selling; in line with Picarelli (1989) we choose for the four main phases.

In the empirical research, the Bales system and the consultative selling approach are being followed to operationalise the mortgage advice process.

Empirical Research

Study

The study was conducted by direct observations in a natural advice setting. In all cases the clients took the initiative for the advice interaction. The conversations took place at the advisor's office. This is the usual procedure. None of the clients objected to tape-recording of the conversation. Their agreement to use the information also for (anonymous) scientific purpose was received afterwards. In total, 142 conversations were observed. Ninety-six conversations recorded only involved pure information transfer and were excluded from the analysis. Forty-six conversations involved advice settings, they were observed and coded. They were all distributed over four mortgage mediators in the regions of Rotterdam and Amsterdam, the Netherlands. Together, these 46 conversations refer to 26 interactions or clients. An interaction is defined as the number of successive conversations between client and advisor necessary to finish the advice process, i.e, including the clients request for an offering. All interactions were successful, meaning that the client requested an offering. The present analysis covers a sample of eight, six, eight and four clients, respectively, of each of the four mortgage mediators. The study observations were carried out in the period of March 22 until October 11, 1990.

Client-advisor conversations were recorded on tape first and typed out later. In this way, an integral and objective description of the actual interaction was obtained [Jorgensen, 1989]. In order to ensure a complete report of the interaction, supplementary questions were asked to the advisor after each conversation. These questions are related to the client, supporting materials such as the computer program and manuals, institutions named, the offering(s), the final mortgage form, and the mortgagee.

Method

Based on the typed reproduction, each sentence/line of the advice interaction was coded using three types of categories:

1) *the person*
   Who is the source of communication, the advisor or the client?
2) *the type of interaction*
   using the twelve categories of Bales presented in Table 3.1
3) *the content regarding mortgage aspects*
   using content categories presented in Table 3.2

Table 3.2   Content categories

DEFINITION OF MAIN CATEGORIES

Information regarding the source
Information evaluating the importance of the reputation of the mortgagee
Information indicating the reliability of the mortgagee or mediator
Explanation of relevant aspects concerning the mortgage product, e.g. mortgage rate, etc.
Review of costs (provision, notary, valuation)
Information indicating the knowledge level of the client
Information that does not involve the mediation process
Data collection concerning the client and answers/spontaneous information provision by the client
Information exchange concerning the course of the mediation, procedures of the mediator and the
   objectives of the interview
Determination of specific wishes of the client
Evaluation of the mortgage/insurance, e.g. too expensive, risky
Information exchange concerning costs and procedures for a house (house yet to be built)
Information concerning a third organisation
Information exchange concerning the territory around the client's house
Information concerning the time period before the mortgage contract starts
Information exchange concerning principles of specific mortgage forms
Explanation of the final amount to be paid at the end of the loan period
Information exchange concerning insurance principles
Information concerning the present mortgage
Explanation of parts of the offering (if requested by the client)
Discussion of the offering after it has been provided

While the Bales interaction categories are generally recommended for coding parts of *problem solving* in dyadic interactions, we also wanted to gain information on the exact contents of the interactions, for example prices, mortgage form, offering, and so on. A qualitative study was conducted to identify relevant aspects that play a role in the advice interaction process. Results of the inquiry were used to develop the present coding system. All interactions were coded using the content categories (see Table 3.2).

According to the sequence of the four consultative selling phases [Picarelli, 1989], we assume that different aspects concerning the content of mortgage advice should be emphasised in each phase. The theoretical expectations regarding the occurrence of the content categories are presented in Table 3.3. In the analysis, these expectations provided the specific research hypotheses.

Table 3.3 Categories per consultative selling phase

CONTENT CATEGORIES RELATED TO PHASES IN CONSULTATIVE SELLING

Phase 1: Establish rapport and confirm objectives
- Information exchange concerning the course of the mediation, procedures of the mediator and the objectives of the interview

Phase 2: Probe for information and listen for/determine clients needs
- Data collection concerning the client and answers/spontaneous information provision by the client
- Determination of specific client wishes
- Evaluation of present mortgage, e.g. too expensive, risky, in the case the client already is mortgage owner
- Information exchange concerning costs and procedures for a house (house yet to be built)

Phase 3: Present programme
- Information exchange concerning principles of specific mortgage forms
- Evaluation of suggested mortgage(s), e.g. expensive, cheap
- Explanation of relevant aspects concerning the mortgage product, e.g. mortgage rate, etc.
- Explanation of the final amount to be paid at the end of the loan period
- Information exchange concerning insurance principles

Phase 4: Resolve objections, close the sale or establish next steps
- Review of costs (provision, notary, valuation)
- Explanation of parts of the offering (when required by client)
- Discussion of the offering after it has been provided

Not all content categories can be related to specific phases of the consultative selling sequence. In phase 1, the content categories that have to do with information exchange concerning the mediation procedures and objectives, are expected to occur according to the consultative selling approach. In phase 2, we expect the categories dealing with data collection and specific wishes concerning the client, information concerning a (new) house, and the present mortgage, to occur. In phase 3, the categories dealing with information concerning mortgage principles, insurance principles, and product aspects are assumed to occur. In phase 4, we expect that the content categories concerning a cost review and offering will occur. The other content categories may occur in different consultative selling phases.

Results

The problem-solving analysis of the mortgage advice interaction focuses on the following issues:
1) type and content of interaction messages (Tables 3.4 and 3.5)
2) differences between advisors (Tables 3.6 and 3.7)
3) sequence of problem-solving phases (Table 3.8)

Type and Content of Interaction Messages

Table 3.4 shows that the main part (73%) of the advice interactions consisted of messages that 'give orientation' and 'give opinion'. Based on the underlying types of problems defined by Bales, almost three-quarters of these processes were only concerned with 'problems of orientation' and 'problems of evaluation'; in fact, these are supposed to provide the groundwork for effective communication [Willett and Pennington, 1966]. Remarkably, less than 6% of the advice interactions occurred by uttering positive tension. The ratios of client to advisor contribution (CL/ADV ratio) are below 1 for all four Bales main categories, indicating that the advisor has the largest share of the conversation.

Table 3.4   Division of Bales' categories

DIVISION OF BALES' CATEGORIES

	Total	%	CL/ADV ratio
Positive Rewards			0.63 (**)
Shows solidarity	272	2	0.12 (**)
Shows tension release	87	0.65	0.56
Agrees	415	3.1	1.25 (**)
Attempted Answers			0.32 (**)
Gives suggestion	785	5.9	0.17 (**)
Gives opinion	4391	33	0.33 (**)
Gives orientation	5359	40	0.33 (**)
Questions			0.66 (**)
Asks for orientation	1192	8.9	0.50 (**)
Asks for opinion	604	4.5	1.05 (**)
Asks for suggestion	34	0.26	1.43 (**)
Negative Reactions			0.76 (**)
Disagrees	130	0.97	1.13 (**)
Shows tension	34	0.25	0.55
Shows antagonism	38	0.29	0.19
	13341	100	

CL/ADV ratio: ratio of client to advisor contribution

Source	
Advisor	72.5%
Client	27.5%
CL/ADV ratio	0.38

(**) significantly different from 1, p<.001

Generally, the advisors contributed almost three times as much to the joint communication as clients. Yet on the categories level, clients showed higher frequencies on the categories 'asking for an opinion', 'asking for a suggestion' (both in the task area), 'agreeing' and 'disagreeing' (both in the emotional area). In our opinion, this clearly demonstrates the uncertainty and the dependent position of the client in mortgage mediation. The average frequency of content categories in the advice interactions is presented in Table 3.5.

Table 3.5 Survey of content categories

SURVEY OF CONTENT CATEGORIES

	Total	%
The source	125	0.71
The importance of the reputation of the mortgagee	32	0.18
The reliability of the mortgagee or mediator	15	0.09
Relevant aspects concerning the mortgage product, e.g. interest level	7268	41.1
Costs (provision, notary, valuation)	235	1.3
The knowledge level of the client	668	3.4
Information that does not involve the mediation process	1971	11.2
The client and answers/spontaneous information provision by the client	2133	12.1
The course of the mediation, procedures of the mediator and the objectives of the interview	2088	11.8
Specific wishes of the client	159	0.9
Evaluation of the mortgage/insurance, e.g. too expensive, risky	777	4.4
Costs and procedures for a house (house yet to be built)	577	3.3
A third organisation	503	2.9
The territory around the clients house	62	0.35
The time period before the mortgage contract starts	38	0.22
Principles of specific mortgage forms	411	2.3
The final amount to be paid at the end of the loan period	30	0.17
Insurance principles	58	0.33
The present mortgage	18	0.1
Parts of the offering (when the client requires one)	221	1.3
Discussion of the offering after it has been provided	258	1.5
	17647	100

Thus, information explaining aspects of the product, for example the amount of the loan, type of mortgage, etc., covered the main part of the advice communication (41%). The small amount of attention given to 'specific wishes of the client' (0.9%) indicates that the emphasis in the advice processes is on product selling, rather than on determining the underlying needs of the client, which is the base for consultative selling. Proportionally, the communication aspects, meant to exchange information concerning the mediation course, procedures, and objectives of the conversation, seems to be reasonably covered in the advice process (11.8%). However, offering aspects only shows to take place in a very small part of the entire interaction (1.5+1.3 =2.8%).

Differences between Advisors
Significant differences between advisors in type of communication appear only regarding the (Bales) categories 'gives suggestion' and 'gives opinion' (see Table 3.6). Regardless of the client or specific situation, some advisors seem to be more dominant in expressing their thoughts than others. In Table 3.6, few significant differences appear between advisors in the content of advice communications.

Regarding the three categories 'specific wishes of the client', 'information exchange concerning house' and 'information exchange concerning insurance' patterns between advisors are different. The second and third of these categories are not necessarily controlled by the advisor. These differences might well be explained by client characteristics. The category 'specific wishes of the client' seems to be controlled by the advisors. The extent to which the advisors try to determine the wishes and needs of a specific client, which we expect to be the key to successful interaction outcomes for the client, was dependent of the advisor. The length of the conversations, in terms of the number of coded sentences/lines, as well as the relative contribution by client and advisor to the advice process also differs significantly between the advisors.

Table 3.6 Differences between advisors (ANOVA)

	p-value of F
Type of communication	
Gives suggestion	<0.033
Gives opinion	<0.040
Communication content	
Specific wishes of the client	<0.022
Information concerning the house	<0.006
Information concerning insurance	<0.001
Length of conversations	<0.001
Relative contribution to the advice process	<0.001

So far, our findings concern similar patterns of content and types of messages underlying the mortgage advice process. When looking at each of the four advisors separately, differences appear (Table 3.7).

In Table 3.7 the four advisors are compared on a number of characteristics. The degree to which the specific wishes of clients are probed for by the different advisors, shows low scores for all advisors: from complete zero to only 2.3 per cent of the conversation content dealt with these personal wishes. The ratio of client - advisor contribution to the conversations show scores range from 0.26 to 0.61. The advisors are doing most of the talking although the differences indicate style differences. Advisor 1 usually has only one conversation per interaction, while advisors 3 and 4 usually need two meetings per client. The length of the interactions reveal remarkable differences in approach between the advisors: advisor 1 has usually only one short conversation in which he does most of the talking with no variance between his clients. He seems to follow a standardised procedure in which the client does not have much of a role. Advisor 2 shows differences between clients in Bales' categories 2, 4 and 11 from Table 3.1, indicating differences in atmosphere between conversations. Advisor 3 seems to adopt most to his clients' wishes and varies most between clients. Neverthelessm he seems to be quite efficient in terms of total interaction length. Advisor 4 needs three to four times as much time as the others, although the communication content does not vary with the client. He either tells it all or does not really adapt to his clients' situation and wishes. These large differences indicate style differences as well as differences in advice approach.

Table 3.7 Advice pattern per advisor (ANOVA)

Advisor	1	2	3	4
Specific wishes of the client	0	1.4	2.3	0.7
Client-advisor contribution	0.29	0.61	0.47	0.26
Length of conversation	156	281	126	647
(N)	5	12	15	10
Length of interaction	196	421	235	1078
(N)	4	8	8	6

Significant differences in the advice pattern between clients per advisor

Type of communication				
Bales acts	no	4	3	1
Bales categories	no	2 11	4 6 7 10	1 2 3 4 6 8 11
Communication content	no	Aspects	• Information concerning mortgage form • Data of client • Information concerning mediation procedure	No
Length of interaction	no	yes	no	no
Client-advisor contribution	no	no	yes	yes

Sequence of Problem-Solving Phases

Exact line numbers of the communication aspects were coded. Knowing the line positions of content aspects in the advice interaction, we tested the observed sequence of advice content categories against the expected sequence of content categories in the consultative selling approach (Table 3.3). We therefore first computed the relative line position for each sentence by dividing the exact line number of the coded category by the highest (last) line number of the same total interaction. Thus the relative position of a category per respondent was found. The average of each content category over all interactions was then computed. These means were then compared with the means of content categories that are expected to occur in each of the four problem-solving phases, for example the means of 'procedures (phase 1); 'data client' (phase 2); 'product and mortgage information' (phase 3) and 'offering (phase 4) (see Table 3.8).

Table 3.8 Mean relative line position scores (*) of content categories expected per phase

expected phase	content categories	relative line position
2	data client	.38
3	mortgage information	.41
2	house information	.46
3	product information	.48
4	costs	.49
3	evaluation	.51
1	procedures	.55
2	client wishes	.56
4	offering	.66

(*) max= at the very end= 1
(*) min= at the very beginning= 0

If all of the content category codes on, for example, data of clients occured in the very beginning of the conversation, the score in Table 3.8 would be near to zero. If, on the other hand, the information on the client was collected at the end, the mean line position score would be near to one. Table 3.8 shows the actual sequence of content categories in the advice interaction. A difference in Table 3.8 in mean line position of .03 or larger is statistically significant at a $p < .05$. Therefore the line positions of a category over all observations are pair-wise compared with the line positions of the other categories. T-tests on these differences show a p-value below .05 for every difference of .03. The position of 'data client' is .38, the lowest of all phases of the conversation. By comparing the mean relative line position of the content categories with other mean relative line positions as expected to occur per problem-solving phase, the relative position of each category in the interactions can be found. The findings from Table 3.8 indicate that the advisors generally start with collecting client's data, followed by providing information about mortgages to their clients. Next, mediation procedures are reviewed, and finally the offering is discussed. Insofar as the advisors probed for client wishes concerning mortgages (see also Table 3.7), the relative position scores in Table 3.8 indicate that 'client wishes' (line position .56) occur after the various product aspects (.41 to .46), 'costs' (.49) and 'procedures about the mediation' (.55) are discussed. The client information that is provided in the beginning is mostly restricted to personal data. Apparently, the advice interactions do not seem to follow an extensive problem-solving sequence, but rather a hard selling approach (with a certain logic of its own). In the consultative selling approach client needs and wishes are the basis for good advice and should be determined in the beginning of the interaction after objectives and procedures have been made clear to the client. Only when sufficient information is gathered about client wishes does the advisor communicate content aspects that ensure a good match between the product offered and client needs.

Discussion and Implications

Actual interactions between client and advisor were observed and tape-recorded. Sequential analysis was carried out after each line/sentence in the advice interaction had been coded. Findings indicate that the mortgage advisors actually behaved more as 'hard-sellers' and do not follow a problem-solving sequence. The approach followed by the advisors most resembles a hard selling approach by first introducing the product, giving almost no attention to client wishes and very little adaption to individual cases. Surprisingly, when the advisors, all of whom volunteered for the study, were asked how they give mortgage advice, they indicated that they act as good problem solvers using consultative selling. At the time of the study, these advisors knew they were being observed. Assuming that in such a situation they will try even harder to function as good advisors, they still show more of a hard-selling than a consultative selling approach. In reality, one can expect the advisors to act even more as hard-sellers. Considering that what they say is different from what they actually do, observation seems to be a promising method to gain further insight into the financial advice process. Once we are able to register what is actually happening between client and advisor we will gain further insight into what aspects of advice behaviour require training and improvement. More research is required to evaluate the real advice process in practice and relate process characteristics to performance characteristics. The assumption that the advice process should follow a problem-solving approach can then be more fully tested.

Bales' system has often been recommended in the literature [Rogers and Farace, 1975; Angelmar and Stern, 1978] to operationalise sequential steps in a problem-solving interaction. However, in this study the Bales coding system does not differentiate, nor does it show the differences found by using coding categories based on consultative selling. The consultative selling model differentiates sequential phases that offer perspectives for future research. Here only part of the consultative selling approach was operationalised, i.e., content aspects present in the four main phases. Future research should also focus on transitions or subphases in the consultative selling model in the analysis.

The increasing significance of the personal advisor function in consumer banking necessitates analysis of client-advisor behaviour in the advice process. The strategic focus on establishing long-term client relationships leads to advisors behaving more as professional problem solvers, for example consultative sellers, trying to provide information that is helpful to the customer [Chevalier, 1993]. In their relational role, advisors will have to balance short-term effectiveness against success in the long run. In the present analysis, no external measures for effectiveness were included. For practical and financial reasons it was not possible to follow clients over time to gather useful information. In follow-up research, different effectiveness measures will be of importance. We suggest to distinguish between at least four measures: contract/offering (short-term overt), client satisfaction (short-term covert), cross-selling (long-term overt) and client loyalty (long-term covert). Research is needed to explore relations between advice approaches and these different measures of success [Greve, Frambach and Verhallen, 1995].

References

Angelmar and Stern, 1978, 'Development of a Content Analytic System for Analysis of Bargaining Communication in Marketing', *Journal of Marketing Research*, 15 (February), pp. 93-102.

Bagozzi, R.P., 1978, 'Salesforce Performance and Satisfaction as a Function of Individual Difference, Interpersonal and Situational Factors', *Journal of Marketing Research*, 15 (November), pp. 517-531.

Bales, R.F., 1950, *Interaction Process Analysis: A Method for the Study of Small Groups*, Reading, Mass.: Addison-Wesley Press.

Campbell, N.C.G., J.L. Graham, A. Jolibert and H.G. Meissner, 1988, 'Marketing Negotiations in France, Germany, the United Kingdom, and the United States', *Journal of Marketing*, 52 (April), pp. 49-62.

Capon, N., 1975, 'Persuasive Effects of Sales Messages Developed from Interaction Process Analysis', *Journal of Business Administration*, 60 (April), pp. 238-244.

Chapple, D. Eliot and Donald Gordon Jr., 1947, 'An Evaluation of Department Store Sales People by the Interaction Chronograph', *Journal of Marketing*, 12, pp. 173-185.

Chevalier, D., 1993, 'The salesperson as consultant', *The American Salesman*, 38 (11), pp. 22-24.

Creeth, R., 1989, 'Apply Consultative Selling to Expand Your Consulting Practice', *Computers in Accounting*, 5 (6), pp. 62-65.

Engel J.F, R.D. Blackwell and D.T. Kollat, 1978, *Consumer Behaviour*, Chicago: The Dryden Press.

Evans, F., 1963, 'Selling as a Dyadic Relationship. A New Approach', *American Behavioral Scientist*, 6, May, p. 76.

Farley, J. and R. Swinth, 1967, 'Effects of Choice and Sales Message on Customer-Salesman Interaction', *Journal of Applied Psychology*, 51 (April), pp. 107-110.

Granger, R.H., 1988, 'Selling, Not Closing, The Key', *National Underwriter*, 92 (17), pp. 67-69.

Greve, H.J.M, R.T. Frambach and Th.M.M. Verhallen, 1995, 'Effective Financial Advice', working paper, Tilburg University.

Hanan, M., 1988, 'How to Become Consultative', *Agency Sales Magazine*, 18 (2), pp. 56-66.

Hubbard, J., 1988, 'How to Make Better Sales Calls', *ABA Banking Journal*, 80 (10), pp. 78-82.

Hulbert, J. and N. Capon, 1972, 'Interpersonal Communication in Marketing: An Overview', *Journal of Marketing Research*, 9, pp. 27-34.

Iacobucci, D. and N. Hopkins, 1992, 'Modelling Dyadic Interactions and Networks in Marketing', *Journal of Marketing Research*, 29 (February), pp. 5-17.

Johnston, W.J and T.V Bonoma, 1984, 'The effect of Power Differences on the Outcome of Consumer Bargaining Situations', *Advances in Consumer Research*, 11.

Jorgensen, D.L., 1989, *Participant Observation, A Methodology for Human Studies*, Newbury Park, CA: Sage Publications.

Keenan, W., 1993, 'Person-to-person', Sales & Marketing Management, 145 (15), pp. 29-30.

McGrath, J.E and J.W. Julian, 1963, 'Interaction Process and Task Outcome in Experimentally - Created Negotiation Groups', *Journal of Psychological Studies*, 14, September, pp. 117-138.

Olhavsky, R.W., 1973, 'Customer-Salesmen Interaction in Appliance Retailing', *Journal of Marketing Research*, 10 (May), pp. 208-212.

Pennington, A., 1968, 'Customer-Salesmen Bargaining Behaviour in Retail Transactions', Journal of Marketing Research, 8 (November), pp. 501-504.

Picarelli, R., 1989, 'The Consultative Selling Technique', *The American Salesman*, 34, (9), pp. 6-8.

Rogers, L.E and R.V. Farace, 1975, 'Analysis of Relational Communication in Dyads: New measurement procedures', *Human Communication Research*, 1 (June), pp. 222-239.

Smith, A., 1991, 'Consultative Selling initiating the Sales Partnership', *The American Salesman*, 36, (1), pp. 3-6.

Soldow, G.F and G.P. Thomas, 1984, 'Relational Communication: Form versus Content in the Sales Interaction', *Journal of Marketing*, 48 (Winter), pp. 84-93.

Solomon, M.R., C. Surprenant, J.A. Czepiel and E.G. Gutman, 1985, 'A Role Theory Perspective on Dyadic Interactions: The Service Encounter', *Journal of Marketing*, 49 (Winter), pp. 99-111.

Spiro, R.L and W.D. Perreault, Jr., 1979, 'Influence Used by Industrial Salespeople: Influence Strategy Mixes and Situational Determinants', *Journal of Business*, 59 (July), pp. 435-455.

Stafford, M.R., 1992, 'Participant observation and the pursuit of truth: Methodological and ethical considerations', *Journal of the Market Research Society*, 35, 1, pp. 63-77.

Webster, F.E., 1968, 'Interpersonal Communication and Salesman Effectiveness', *Journal of Marketing*, 32 (July), pp. 7-13.

Weitz, B.A., 1978, 'The Relationship between Salesperson Performance and Understanding of Customer Decision Making', *Journal of Marketing Research*, 15 (November), pp. 501-516.

Weitz, B.A., 1981, 'Effectiveness in Sales Interactions: A Contingency Framework', *Journal of Marketing*, 45 (Winter), pp. 85-103.

Willett, R.P. and A.L. Pennington, 1966, 'Customer and Salesman: The Anatomy of Choice and Influence in a Retail Setting', *Science Technology and Marketing*, pp. 598-616.

Williams, K.C. and R.L. Spiro, 1985, 'Communication Style in the Salesperson-Customer Dyad', *Journal of Marketing Research*, 12 (November), pp. 434-442.

Williams, K.C, R.L. Spiro and L.M. Fine, 1990, 'The Customer-Salesperson Dyad: An Interaction/Communication Model and Review', *Journal of Personal Selling and Sales Management*, 10 (Summer), pp. 29-43.

4

Customer Participation and Customer Satisfaction

Frédéric Marion[1]

Previous research has underlined that customer participation can be part of customer satisfaction. This article analyses the link between customer participation and customer satisfaction using three case studies. The main result is that cooperation is an important condition for customer participation.

Introduction

The degree of customer participation in the service process is one of the most fundamental characteristics of a service. As a result of the difficulty of separating simultaneous production and consumption of a service, customer participation plays a very important role in the process of evaluating satisfaction by the customer. This led Lehtinen [1983] to distinguish the quality of the process from the result, a theory taken up by Grönroos [1986] in his model for evaluating perceived service quality.

Grönroos even suggests that the service should be seen as a process, involving multiple interactions between the customer and the service company. Berry, Zeithaml and Parasuraman [1985: 46] had previously pointed out that customer participation would contribute to the customer experience.

Previous work has shown that customers can have a greater or lesser desire to participate [Langeard, Bateson, Lovelock and Eiglier, 1981: 33]. Furthermore, for some authors, customer participation raises various problems for the service delivery process [Chase, 1978 and 1981] and, consequently, causes greater difficulty in managing and controlling service quality.

The aim of this article is to assess the link between customer participation and customer satisfaction. After a synthesis of existing material, we will present the main

---

1   Frédéric Marion is a research fellow at the Institut de Recherche de l'Entreprise (IRE), the research centre of the Lyon Graduate School of Business, France.

results of empirical research in three case studies on the consequences of customer participation for the evaluation of the service process.

Customer Participation and Satisfaction: An Analysis of Existing Material

Although research on customer participation is limited, it offers some invaluable information on the links that exist between customer participation and satisfaction.

Participation, Customer Behaviour and Understanding the Process

According to Chase [1978 and 1981], the process is harder to control when customer participation is high. Customer participation in the service process raises different, yet closely related issues concerning the delivery process of a service by the supplier:

* the difficulty of controlling the role and, in particular, the behaviour of the customer;
* the complexity of controlling and managing productivity and/or the costs of the service process;
* the difficulty of controlling the quality of the service offered.

Chase's suggestion is to decouple the *technical core* from environmental influences, such as customer contact, if possible. To increase productivity, Mills, Chase and Margulies [1983: 308] add that, when their presence is required in the service process, customers may be viewed as *'partial' employees*.

The limits of such an operation have since been revealed. Chase, who defines the degree of contact as the "customer contact time / service creation time" ratio, puts forward the theory that the control and organisation of a service is more difficult as this ratio increases. Wemmerlöv [1984: 10-11; and 1991] and Schmenner [1986: 24], assuming that the concept of customer contact refers to totally different situations which have to be distinguished, prefer to take into account customer *intervention* or *interaction* (meaning active intervention) with the staff/equipment or technology (Wemmerlöv). This distinction is also based on the degree of control of the supplier during the process: a service with significant customer contact time can be totally controlled (for example, a hotel) and, consequently, more efficient than one having a low contact time.

Langeard *et al.* [1981] have approached this issue from a different angle. In their analysis of the behaviour of customers who were asked to choose between a process involving little participation and another involving significant participation in the same service, they demonstrated how individuals behave differently depending on different levels of participation. On the basis of their findings concerning elements which in their view are important in customer participation, they distinguished two types of customers: *active managers* and *passive customers*. For *active managers* these elements include time — because service activities are increasingly limited by strict time budgets [see also Bateson, 1985] — and the control of the situation. For *passive customers* they include the physical or mental effort needed, and the risks involved, i.e., fulfilling the service without incident. Eiglier and Langeard [1987: 44] conclude:

"Firstly, we must test the reactions of the most active customers by concentrating on the time spent and the control of the situation. Secondly, we must involve the most passive customers by showing them that the effort needed is minimal and the risks non-existent".

On the basis of this literature, it is likely that customer cooperation has an influence on customer satisfaction which can differ between customer segments.

Participation, Cooperation and Satisfaction

Lovelock and Young wrote, as early as 1977, that it is necessary to obtain customer cooperation when their participation is needed. Eiglier and Langeard [1987: 33] point out that a customer may wish to increase his participation depending upon the service in question, or may simply wish to participate for various reasons:

"His education tells him that he could carry out a certain number of tasks which do not seem very complicated. His experience tells him not to expect a miracle from someone carrying out repetitive and monotonous tasks, and therefore poorly motivated. Finally, his professional life-style can reflect on his personal life-style, for example, he may wish to act, rather than wait, or may do it himself to reduce any doubts he may have".

According to Eiglier and Langeard, participation can be justified not only because of economic reasons, but also for marketing reasons, mainly through greater customer independence.

Eiglier, Bateson, Langeard and Lovelock [1979: 8] point out that awareness of participation, or increased customer participation, requires some kind of compensation to obtain cooperation. According to Eiglier *et al.*, this compensation can be given in three ways: a reduced price or time-saving (or a combination of these two types) for the same service, or improved service quality. Lovelock and Young [1977: 115-116; 1979: 177], however, point out that the different types of compensation generally offered affect at least one of the elements of marketing mix. Our first observations lead us to a number of additional comments [Marion, 1991 : 18-24]: we prefer to speak of cost, rather than price reduction. (A service is generally considered by a company customer not simply as a product to be bought, but as an utility which has a cost.) We also add to the list a reduction in the possible risks of not obtaining the desired result (as a direct result of the service or as a result of its utilisation in the long term), less effort involved (because, for example, service provision will be quicker and therefore allow for a better utilisation of the service by simplifying the tasks usually performed), or the fact that the participant is affectively of intellectually interested in participating in a service process.

Conditions for Customer Participation

Lovelock and Young [1977: 175] and, later, Lehtinen [1985: 117], emphasise the need for customer training, an idea taken up by Eiglier *et al.* [1979: 7] who refer to "rules *or standards to be respected*", and Mills *et al.* [1983: 305] who opt for "*imposed behavioural standards*". Another condition which, without being directly mentioned in the literature, should be taken into consideration is customer availability, which is considered a time dimension in the typology of Langeard *et al.* [1981].

This study aims to come to a better understanding of customer participation in the service provision and its influence on the efficiency of the process in terms of both economic performance for the supplier and satisfaction for the customer. Therefore, we will examine under what circumstances customer participation can be efficient. Whereas previous work has dealt only with individual customer participation, we will study a situation involving a company customer.

The hypothesis can be re-formulated as follows: the process of a given service, which needs an (expected) low customer participation, has an efficiency considered as basic efficiency and is recorded as zero efficiency. For the same type of service, the efficiency of a process calling for significant participation will vary depending on the conditions with respect to this participation:

- low participation => efficiency = 0;
- higher participation without conditions => decreasing efficiency;
- higher participation with conditions => increasing efficiency.

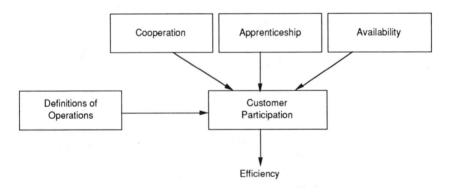

Figure 4.1 Conditions for customer participation

Analysis of previous research has led us to formulate more precise hypotheses which are based around the idea that the efficiency of a process involving a significant level of customer participation depends on the triad (cooperation - apprenticeship - availability) of the customer, as shown in Figure 4.1 [Marion, 1991:22, and 1992:17]. We consider customer cooperation, apprenticeship and availability conditions that are able to explain the contribution of customer participation to the efficiency of the process, seen in terms of both economic performance for the supplier and satisfaction in the eyes of the customer. These concepts are defined as follows:

- cooperation is the actual customer willingness to perform operations upon demand;
- apprenticeship is the result of the process that shows customers what they are expected to do and how they should do it;
- availability is the time the customer can spend doing what he is asked to do.

Our research into conditions for customer participation in the service provision has led us to explore and investigate the link between customer participation and customer satisfaction.

Research Design

To test our hypotheses and analyse the conditions for customer participation, we have carried out research in three companies: two computer services companies and a catering firm. Subsequently, we have made detailed descriptions of 16 cases within these three companies, in which customers play an important role:

- the service offered to six customers of the first computer services company, involving the 'installation of an accounts control business package';
- the service 'accounting data output' to four different accounts departments in a customer company to the second computer services company;
- the service offered by the catering firm to six restaurants, two straightforward cafeterias and four buffet restaurants. The expected customer participation differs between these two types of self-service restaurants.

The research in each company involved the planning of a first step which enabled us:

- to identify the service to be analysed, bearing in mind the objectives and limits of the project;
- to define the service and describe the different operations involved, while at the same time identifying the different types of possible customer participation;
- to define the performance indicators relevant to the analysis.

In order to gather all information required for the detailed description of each case, we either interviewed contact personnel of the supplier or asked them to complete a questionnaire. In a number of cases both methods were used. Furthermore, we interviewed 112 employees of the customer companies about a number of items, including satisfaction: 81 users of the cafetarias of the catering firm, 10 decision makers and/or users of the service of the first computer services company, and 21 of the second.

Results

By analysing possible conditions for customer participation that could influence the overall service performance (i.e., both economic performance for the supplier and customer satisfaction), the research resulted in a number of conclusions concerning the link between customer participation and satisfaction.

Generally, the results show that, in order to define the operations to be realised with or by the customer, several parameters linked to the nature of the operation and to the characteristics of the activity must be taken into consideration. Conditions governing this participation should not be neglected here. Overall performance concerning service provision should be generally acceptable, depending not only on the level of customer participation, but also on the associated conditions of cooperation, apprenticeship and availability.

We will now look at the results in the more precise context of the link between customer participation and customer satisfaction. If customer cooperation seems to be an important condition for customer satisfaction, a very important linked result is that cooperation can be only in the benefits the customer will derive from the service, but not in the process of providing the service.

Cooperation in the Process versus Cooperation in the Benefits of the Service Provision

As previously mentioned, our research is concerned with inter-organisational service relationships. This has led us to measure levels of cooperation, apprenticeship, availability and satisfaction for different employees serving the same customer, in order to evaluate the company on each of these concepts.

If the levels of apprenticeship and availability can influence the economic performance of the service for the supplier, our observations do not allow us to say whether they leave the customer dissatisfied. This does not hold true for the condition of cooperation: although few of those interviewed declared not to have adhered to the proposed process and the participation expected of them, it is possible to make a number of assertions concerning the link between customer cooperation and satisfaction.

Of the 112 people interviewed, only eight said that they had not been cooperative and/or were not satisfied. These eight respondents were all users of the catering firm's service. Customers of the computer services companies all said they had been cooperative and were satisfied with the service. The 112 people interviewed can be categorised as follows:

Table 4.1 Customer cooperation and customer satisfaction

	Cooperation	No cooperation	Total
Satisfaction	104	5	109
Dissatisfaction	2	1	3
Total	106	6	112

From Table 4.1 we cannot draw any other definite conclusions. However, a number of observations can be made on an individual basis.

Two people that were dissatisfied despite following the process used two different catering facilities (a straightforward canteen for the first and a buffet canteen for the second), and they blamed their dissatisfaction on poor food quality. Thus, to adhere to the process does not guarantee customer satisfaction. At the same time, not adhering to the process is not necessarily synonymous with dissatisfaction, as shown by the examples of the five people who said they had not adhered to the process but were satisfied with the service. In these cases, the benefits derived from the service, in a situation where customers are satisfied with the quality in relation to these benefits (in a company canteen this generally means: good food in sufficient quantities, fast service and a friendly atmosphere) are considered as being more important than the process itself and expected customer participation in this process.

The person who said she had not adhered to the system and who was not satisfied with the service is equally important. This 45 year old employee used to eat in a straightforward self-service cafeteria. The company restaurant about which she was interviewed is a large buffet restaurant serving almost 2,000 meals a day on the basis of what is called the multi-choice concept, with a separate salad bar, meat, grill, fish, pizzas, cheese, sweets, and so on. Dissatisfied with the service, she judged that the quality of the food and the ambience were inadequate while it was very important to her. Finally, she compared the restaurant with the one she used to visit, by saying that the latter was "less chaotic", better organised, friendlier and simply better.

This case seems to demonstrate that, through the provision of a service, customers discriminate between two aspects: the benefits derived from the service (for example: good food, fast service, a friendly atmosphere for a company restaurant), and the way the service is given, i.e., the process and expected customer participation in this process. Thus, customers typically attach a varying degree of importance to the process:

- the importance they attach to participation may be lower than the importance they attach to the benefits to be derived from the service: therefore customers could be satisfied with the service, even if the participation required by the supplier is not equal to the participation expected by themselves;

- the importance they attach to participation may be equal to the importance they attach to the benefits to be derived from the service; thus, they risk being dissatisfied with the service if the participation required by the supplier is not equal to the participation expected by themselves.

Hence, we propose to distinguish customer cooperation in the service process according to the benefits to be drawn from the service, from customer cooperation in the actual operations. When managing customer participation it is necessary to check that, although a person seems cooperative, he may be unwilling to perform certain specific operations, which might cause a problem. This concern is all the more worrying because the customer does not always know in advance what the participation expected of him exactly consists of. In fact, it is not always clear what is expected of the customer; this sometimes depends on unknown parameters before starting the process.

Motivation for Cooperation

We asked the people we interviewed what motivated them to participate. Table 4.2. indicates the sources of motivation within the two computer services companies (CSC 1 and 2) and the catering firm (CF).

Table 4.2   Cooperation and sources of motivation

	Improvement of service quality	Time-saving	Better use of the benefits gained from the service
CSC 1			
Case 1	+	-	-
Case 2	+	-	-
Case 3	+	-	-
Case 4	+	+	-
Case 5	+	-	-
Case 6	+	+	-
CSC 2			
Case 7	+	-	+
Case 8	+	-	-
Case 9	+	-	+
Case 10	+	-	+
CF			
Case 11	+	+	+
Case 12	+	+	+
Case 13	+	+	+
Case 14	+	+	+
Case 15	+	+	+
Case 16	+	+	-

One source of motivation was mentioned in each case: participation is linked to improved service quality. This *compensation* [see also Lovelock and Young, 1977: 115-116; Eiglier *et al.*, 1979: 8], comes in different forms depending on the context: it can be the ambience of the (straightforward or buffet) canteen, the freedom of choice and movement, the possibility of taking one's time or of taking as much or as little as desired (buffet system), checking what has been gained from the training period, and maximising (afterwards) the knowledge acquired from the installation of the business software package.

A number of advantages created by participation and ensuring customer cooperation varied from time-saving to an easier use of the benefits gained from the service. Since this research was essentially concerned with users of the service, cost-saving (or price for an individual rather than a company) was not mentioned spontaneously as an advantage. It would undoubtedly have been considered an important element by the company decision makers.

In regard to the benefits actually obtained, we would like to underline the perceived benefits of customer participation. We have analysed the cases involving the installation of accounting business software package systems normally expected to save the operators (as well as the installer) time as a result of having prepared the installation and operator availability during the installation itself. However, time-saving was perceived in only two out of the six cases analysed. Reasons why users did not experience time-saving in the other four cases included inadequate preparation (by users), and/or inadequate user availability during installation.

Past experience is also an important factor when explaining user behaviour. This is very clear, for example, in the case of the second computer services company analysed. The 21 people interviewed working for customers of this company all said they had been cooperative: all of them had experience with processing accounts, with the same supplier and with the old version of the software package, so they knew their participation in the production of data would be beneficial to them.

Thus, we might conclude that past experience reduces risks with respect to the purchase of the service. For example, it can be less efficient than expected, difficult to use, more expensive than expected, and so on. It enables customers to control their own participation: their experience endows them with a mastery of the service and its process, they know what is expected of them, which will enable them, as co-producers, to optimise the benefits to be gained from the service.

Conclusion

In this article we have tried to explain the link between customer participation and customer satisfaction. Our research has shown the importance of conditions of cooperation, apprenticeship and availability to make the overall performance of a service provision acceptable. Further findings from our research can be summarised as follows:

- The management of customer cooperation in the service process and the participation involved is important to the supplier. In fact, in some cases, customers attach equal importance to their participation and to the benefits they will derive from the service. Hence, they risk being dissatisfied with the service if the participation required of them is not equal to the participation expected by themselves. Thus:

  - If customers buying a service seem to adhere to it, they are not always aware of what it may mean in relation to what is required of them. Are they really aware that without their participation the service would not exist?

  - Furthermore, customers may be compensated for their cooperation: one source of motivation mentioned by customers in each case is better service quality due to their own participation; other sources of motivation mentioned are time-saving and an easier use of the benefits gained from the service realised by their participation.

- Past experience with the service is an explanatory factor of user behaviour: it enables customers to control their own participation, because they know what is expected of them and what advantages they can derive from participation.

The main aim of the research presented in this article has been to put forward a number of preliminary conclusions concerning the link between customer participation and customer satisfaction. These findings contribute to understanding the interface between service companies and their customers. It provides a framework in which customer participation can be examined and areas can be identified with poor performance. There are ample opportunities to improve management of customers, not only as simple buyers, but also as co-producers of the service.

References

Bateson, J.E.G., 1985, 'Self-Service Consumer: An Explorary Study', *Journal of Retailing*, 61 (3).

Berry, L.L., V.A. Zeithaml and C.A. Parasuraman, 1985, 'Quality Counts in Services Too', *Business Horizons*, 28 (3), pp.44-52.

Chase, R.B., 1978, 'When Does the Customer Fit in a Service Operation?', *Harvard Business Review*), pp.137-140.

Chase, R.B., 1981, 'The Customer Contact Approach to Services: Theoretical Bases and Practical Extensions', *Operations Research*, 29 (4), pp.686-706.

Eiglier,P., J.E.G. Bateson, E. Langeard and C.H. Lovelock, 1979, 'Participation du Client au Système de 'Servuction': Concepts et Mesure', in Proceedings of the 6th International Marketing Research Seminar, *Marketing des services - Gestion de la distribution*, La Londe des Maures: IAE Aix-en-Provence.

Eiglier, P. et E. Langeard, 1987, *Servuction. Le marketing des services*, Paris: McGraw-Hill.

Grönroos, C.G., 1986 (January), *Developing Service Quality: Some Managerial Implications*, Helsinki: Swedish School of Economics and Business Administration.

Langeard, E., J.E.G. Bateson, C.H. Lovelock and P. Eiglier, 1981, *Services Marketing: New Insights from Consumers and Managers*, Report 81-104, Cambridge, Mass.: Marketing Science Institute.

Lehtinen, J.R., 1983, 'Customer-Oriented Service System', Working Paper, Helsinki: Service Management Institute.

Lehtinen, J.R., 1985, 'Improving Service Quality by Analysing the Service Production Process', in C.G. Grönroos and E. Gummesson (eds.), *Service Marketing: Nordic School Perspectives*, Stockholm: University, Department of Business Administration), pp.110-120.

Lovelock, C.H. and R.F. Young, 1977 (November), 'Marketing's Potential for Improving Productivity in Service Industries', in P. Eiglier, E. Langeard, C.H. Lovelock, J.E.G. Bateson and R.F. Young, *Marketing Consumer Services: New Insights*, Cambridge, Mass.: Marketing Science Institute, pp.105-121.

Marion, F., 1991 (April), 'Impact de la participation du client, quelques concepts et hypothèses', Working Paper 9129 MSE, IRE/Groupe ESC Lyon.

Marion, F., 1992 (June), 'Gestion de la qualité et réalisation du service en milieu interorganisationnel', in *Proceedings of the 2nd International Seminar on Service Activities Management*, La Londe des Maures: IAE Aix-en-Provence), pp.338-357.

Mills, P.K., R.B. Chase and N. Margulies, 1983 (April), 'Motivating the Client/Employee System as a Service Production Strategy', *Academy of Management Review*, 8), pp.301-310.

Schmenner, R.W., 1986 (Spring), 'How Can Service Businesses Survive and Prosper?', *Sloan Management Review*, pp.21-32.

Wemmerlöv, U.n, 1984 (January), 'A Proposed Taxonomy for Service Processes and its Implications for System Design', Working Paper, Graduate School of Business, Madison: University of Wisconsin.

Wemmerlöv, U., 1990, 'A Taxonomy for Service Processes and its Implications for System Design', *International Journal of Service Industry Management*, 1 (3), pp.20-40.

5

Internal Marketing: Interfacing the Internal and External Environments

Richard J Varey[1] and Colin T Gilligan[2]

Managing *for* change offers considerable potential for the development of competitive advantage through evolutionary enhancement of capability which managers *of* change can only follow.

The business organisation is now inevitably a service provider irrespective of whether its output is primarily that of a product or a service. Service quality management is a strategic business technology, as yet only rarely fully understood by those who design and deliver service to internal and external customers.

In complete contrast to a production orientation the abilities and output of the firm are not assumed to be fixed or to change only as the firm desires, but are driven to change by customer preferences. In this way customer satisfaction is the key to competitive performance. *Internal marketing* can ensure that the organisation's adaptive capability (i.e., the capacity for responsive change which requires reduced organisational inertia) in the face of radical changes in the external trading environment is increased substantially. We identify a number of significant changes in the operating environments that will challenge the marketer, and a framework for internal marketing is presented and explored. We discuss how service quality management might be integrated with organisation development and marketing strategy, and provides a mechanism for managing the evolution of the responsive organisation by interfacing the internal environment with the realities of the external environment. The cases of a health service provider and a manufacturing organisation are used to illustrate the application of our conception of *internal marketing*.

Introduction

Business organisations have been described as 'planned economies' where clearly defined activities are co-ordinated towards clearly defined goals. Problems of rigidity, lack of initiative and difficulty of management have prevailed and internal

1   Director of the BNFL Corporate Communications Unit, The Management School, University of Salford, Salford, M5 4WT, United Kingdom.
2   Professor of Marketing, Sheffield Business School, Sheffield Hallam University, Sheffield, S17 4AB, United Kingdom.

market relations have been urged as a solution to ensure that a competitive dynamic internal environment inside the firm can assist it to respond to the competitive dynamic external environment [Gummesson, 1987].

Many believe that as customer expectations are increasing service excellence is becoming a major competitive platform if only because current service is mostly so poor. By consistently meeting or exceeding the expectations of customers some firms are able to change the rules of business competition [Quinn and Humble, 1993].

"Service is the new competitive edge"
[Humble quoted in Quinn and Humble, 1993].

Re-Writing the Competitive Rules

Discussions with managers in a wide range of businesses have revealed some significant challenges for the organisation which wishes to build and maintain a strong competitive position in the 1990s.

Table 5.1 Challenges to traditional marketing

Traditional markets are stagnating and fragmenting
Domestic and foreign competition is increasing
Product proliferation continues unabated
Consumers are perceiving greater product parity
Product and market lifecycles are shortening
Increasing niche attacks from competitors
Customers are becoming more sophisticated
Price sensitivity is growing
Strong downward price pressures
Promotional costs continue to rise whilst effectiveness declines
The cost of managing a salesforce continues to rise
Patterns of distribution are changing
A general erosion of competitive advantage

Within the organisation, other significant changes are being experienced [Handy, 1989 and 1994; Peters, 1992]:

- the roles of manager and supervisor are changing
- organisations are shedding layers of hierarchy
- the employee-employer relationship is changing
- expectations of working life are changing

Implications for Managers

Managers recognising one or only a few of these changes in their own business environment must take up the challenge and adjust their strategy with evolutionary change. When, as is increasingly the case, the majority of these changes are identified as simultaneously occurring, the need is for a more radical response, and business re-engineering is necessary to align the organisation and its priorities with its market realities. Strategic drift allows a widening gap to grow between what the organisation is doing and what it needs to do, and this requires transformational change to realign the organisation with the demands of the environment.

A truly responsive organisation is required in a dynamic environment if its market position is to be sustained or improved. The traditional view of response to change has been a sequence of steps in diagnosis, planning, implementation, and evaluation. Vail [1989] has suggested that change is turbulent "white water" which requires a fundamentally different management approach. Change in organisations should be viewed as an ongoing complex and dynamic process [Dawson, 1994: 46].

Greater flexibility, in a number of forms [Dawson, 1994: 29], is required to *manage for change* in increasingly unpredictable markets if an effective fit between organisational structure and functional performance is sought [Donaldson, 1987].

Real innovations in the organisation of work are occurring, representing a shift towards a collaborative system of industrial relations and teamwork in which the employee is empowered for self-control. Supervision is being reduced and control responsibility is being devolved to front-line workers as worker and manager interests become overlapped. This requires a new set of values and beliefs, and improves the quality of working life and the manager's ability to adapt production to changing market conditions [Dawson, 1994: 30].

It is over 20 years since it was pointed out that [Pugh, Hickson and Hinings, 1971]:

> "people are one of the essential resources required to achieve (organisation) aims. But people are a rather special sort of resource. They not only work for the organisation, they are the organisation".

Informal and formal networks are replacing hierarchy and an organic organisation is replacing the mechanistic organisation [Burns and Stalker, 1961].

Barriers to Flexible Responsiveness

Given the nature and significance of the environmental changes that are taking place, it is apparent that organisations need to respond in a number of fundamental ways. Without these changes, the problems of strategic drift and organisational inflexibility are likely to be reflected in an increasing distancing from the market. However, our examination of a wide range of management literature and feedback from students and clients suggests that many barriers exist to prevent the 'common sense' of responsive organisation occurring without difficulty. Table 5.2 is an attempt to summarise the major barriers to responsive flexible organisational arrangements; these are illustrated in Figure 5.3.

Table 5.2 Barriers to the responsive flexible organisation

Short-term thinking
A production orientation - customers are not central to decision-making
Managers who act on own 'feelings' without analysis
Lack of timely market intelligence - changes not perceived
Directive, control-oriented management style
Too much analysis, too little action
Rigid inappropriate structures
Confrontational industrial relations
Unclear future direction
Poor inter-functional relations
Attempts to change culture which do not account for internal political processes or
    realistic time frame for change
Participative change strategies which are not participative!
Coercive-resistive working relations between management and workforce
Mechanistic view of organisation
Scale/scope of changes not recognised
Poor co-ordination between functions
Skills gaps
Changes prompt only slow reaction - a lack of proactive changes

Although each of the points in Table 5.2 may well have implications for how the organisation operates, they need to be seen as manifestations of a more fundamental problem, that of managerial attitudes and organisational culture. It follows from this that if the organisation is to make the evolutionary or transformational changes needed to overcome these barriers, fundamental shifts in both attitudes and management practice are needed. An internal customer orientation is required since this can lead to a more responsive orientation towards external customers. What is being advocated is the effective marketing of the marketing concept within the organisation. The role of this internal marketing is to drive the necessary changes in attitude and behaviour in workers and managers alike.

The Importance of Sustainable Competitive Advantage

Competitive advantage means being better than competitors in terms meaningful to customers and exceeding customer expectations so that there is no perceived quality gap [Parasuraman, Zeithaml and Berry, 1988]. The organisation's strengths and its distinctive competencies must match the key success requirements for operating effectively in the target market *and* exceed those of its competitors and be sustainable over time [Brown, 1993].

A sustainable competitive advantage requires a distinctive capability in terms of appropriate resources and their organisation and deployment, including accurate, timely and relevant information as a decision-making resource. Something the organisation does, or how it does it, must be beyond normal competitive dynamics for imitation.

Sources of Competitive Advantage

The bases for building and maintaining a competitive advantage may be comparative differentials of organisation including functional relationships, resources, or relationships with external bodies [adapted from Wilson and Gilligan with Pearson, 1992: 34].

Table 5.3 Sources of competitive advantage

Organisational advantages	Functional/skill/resource advantages	Advantages based on relationships with external bodies
economies of scale	customer base	customer loyalty
flexibility	new product development skills	channel control
competitive stance/position	service support	government assistance
size	communication & advertising	cartels
speed of response	product technology	inter-organisational relationships, including supplier links
financial strength	patents	beneficial tariff and non-tariff trade barriers
reputation	process efficiency experience product quality management-worker relations flexibility of workforce & production processes	

Internal Factors of Sustainable Competitive Advantage

Many of the bases for sustainable competitive advantage are internal advantages of organisation or resources. One source of advantage could be how change is managed. The needs of organisation members and its customers are not constant over time, and the management *of* change is reactive, and introduces a time-lag. Management *for* change is proactive and anticipatory, but requires receptiveness and a high state of readiness for change and an ability to contribute.

Change may be problem-driven, training-driven, or customer-driven [Lawton, 1991]. To create a climate for change it is necessary to give people new roles, responsibilities and relationships in a new organisational context within and across interdependent functions which map the key customer-serving processes and enable and encourage collaborative diagnosis of business problems and consensus for a 'task-aligned' vision of the organisation [Beer, Eisenstat and Spector, 1990]:

> "the purpose of change is to create an asset that did not exist before — a learning organisation capable of adapting to a changing competitive environment".

The resulting organisational arrangements must maintain concern for external influences whilst accommodating internal concerns such as *quality of working life*. Sustainable competitive advantage requires an organisational culture that drives culture modification to maintain culture value, rarity and imperfect imitability [Barney, 1986].

Organisational Capability

Technical capability is concerned with process efficiency, skills, expertise, and resource utilisation. The emergent characteristics of organisation [Checkland and Scholes, 1990] including the capability for change and relational quality [Gummesson, 1987] determine capability for producing appropriate outputs which is not easily imitable. The ability of managers to operationalise service quality is also crucial. Service quality, which has performance and perceptual attributes, includes customer service and customer relations. It is the extent to which the customer is satisfied with the service product, i.e., what the supplier provides the customer with [Lawton, 1991]. Managers must also understand what customer orientation means in operational terms [Berry, Zeithaml and Parasuraman, 1990]:

- effectively competing for good service staff
- emphasis on service teams
- encouraging and facilitating customers to complain, and acting on this
- timely communication with customers, including publicising improvements
- encouraging and facilitating employees to respond to customer problems

Effectiveness in promoting customer/market orientation, i.e., emphasis on matching company objectives and capabilities with the needs and wants of customers, is also crucial. But care is necessary as marketing orientation appears to emphasise customer needs and wants, i.e., company capability may be neglected and not developed [Sharp, 1991]. In practice it must mean that the firm is committed to strategic thinking in adopting a long-run approach to analysing environmental change in the light of its own mission and capabilities. There should be a close match, with synergy, between organisational competencies and market needs, i.e., relevance of the *what* and *how* of the organisation's operations must be a function of the organisation's characteristics and not solely those of the market [Sharp, 1991: 24]. Customers are only one part of a complex environment which includes economic pressures, market structure, competitive action, and employee aspirations. Pure customer orientation does not allow for the task of 'optimal balancing' [Kaldor in Sharp, 1991: 24]. Market orientation emphasises current consumer wants and is about customer expectation management, but managers must also consider the competing expectations of *end users* and other customers, many of whom are inside the organisation [Lawton, 1991].

Marketing capability requires human, market, and organisational assets [Möller and Anttila, 1987] including considerations of the number and competence of marketers, position of the firm in its markets, and effectiveness of marketing operations and degree of integration with other key functions, as well as strategies, policies, plans and programmes developed and acted upon by the firm. Thus there are external and internal domains for marketing capability, including assessing customer and competitor behaviour and managing relationships with customers, competitors, suppliers, and intermediaries; strategic orientation; integration of functions; management of marketing as a function and its position in operational planning and management system of the firm. Given this, the role of marketing can be seen in terms of integration of specialist expertise and functional capabilities and the orchestrator to match these to market needs.

Continuous improvement is a further capability brought about by convergent thinking. An interaction model emphasises 'learning by doing' in recognising the unique experience gains for both parties in building close customer-supplier relationships. Here the customer is the end user and must be the real focus of attention as it is possible to attend to internal customers at the expense of the external end user [Lawton, 1991]. Whilst internal customers can be agents of the end user or of the supplier, i.e., their employer, there can be considerable role ambiguity and conflicts which must be recognised and managed positively. Thus marketing is seen as relationship management which aims to create, develop, and maintain a network in which the firm thrives [Gummesson, 1987].

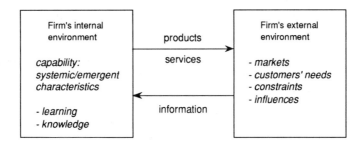

Figure 5.1 Interfacing the internal and external relationships

Organisational boundaries separating customers and the firm become blurred [Ulrich, 1989]. All employees in the business understand and work to meet customer values and there is strategic unity between employees and customers. This requires knowledge of how customers perceive the firm and how closely they match desired perceptions (a "common sensitivity to the market" [Saba quoted in Witcher, 1990: 2]).

Internal Marketing: A Mechanism for Enhancing the Organisation's Capability

Internal marketing has been described as a *holistic management process* [George, 1990] to integrate the multiple functions of the organisation by:

- ensuring that all employees understand and experience the business and its activities in an environment that supports customer consciousness
- ensuring that all employees are prepared and motivated to act in a service-oriented manner

Internal marketing focuses on achieving effective internal exchanges between the organisation and its employee groups as a prerequisite for successful exchanges with external markets [George, 1990]. This helps to enhance and ensure speed and relevance of response to an increasingly complex web of isolated and inter-related factors which constrain, influence, or determine the actions and achievable objectives of the organisation.

The evolution of organisational capability for change and responsiveness must be planned, i.e. driven. Strategy can then be translated into operational reality by a process of "managing ideas into good currency so that innovative ideas are implemented and institutionalised" [Van de Ven, 1986]. Dawson [1994] has suggested that many organisations respond to extreme turbulence in their environments, i.e. unpredictable and rapid changes, by imitating apparently successful others. But imitation cannot be sufficient for sustainable competitive advantage. Managers need a superior culture and organisation management skills. Here we take 'organisation' to mean the web of interconnected relations of a complex range of factors including resources, values and assumptions, i.e. ours is a holistic or systemic view. What is required is real flexibility and adaptability in organising the business. The 'organisation' becomes a collection of project teams that work for each other. Organisational arrangements are not static, fixed, and rigid, but recognise and accommodate the dynamism of their environment.

Organisation development may be associated with the notion of asset-led marketing [Davidson, 1987] where the management task is to improve effectiveness of asset use in the organisation's market(s) and to improve the assets themselves (including organisational relationships and knowledge), thereby building and utilising emergent characteristics of the organisation which may be hard for competitors to identify and imitate.

In operationalising service quality we can think of *Internal Service Quality*, i.e., the quality of strategic decision-making and operational capability through strategic choice deployment; and *External Service Quality:* in which customer expectation management recognises the role of customer perceptions and actively seeks a constantly updated understanding and meeting of the needs by building close relationships with selectively chosen customers. Heskett's *service sector profit chain* [Heskett, 1992] has been useful in making the connection between internal service quality, external service quality, and the organisation's financial performance.

Internal marketing encourages the view that marketing is a process which involves the whole firm as the means by which a match is continuously maintained between its offerings and its customers' needs. Marketing processes are the core activity of the service provider and responsibility for them crosses functional divides [Payne, 1988]. Multi-disciplined self-managing work teams are the most suitable organisational structure to deliver improved quality, responsiveness and customer focus by ensuring ownership and involvement at all levels [Chaudhry-Lawton, Lawton, Murphy and Terry 1992; Tjosvold, 1992; Wellins, Byham and Wilson 1991]. Indeed, Peters [1992] suggests that it is necessary to go beyond this arrangement to *'self-contained' work groups*. Teams make their own plans for implementing strategy to which they have contributed market appraisal information in a structured iterative planning process which recognises that responsibility for strategic moves should be at the customer interface. The decision-making process is pushed down to the level where the information is available, and the teams re-organise their work to ensure appropriate process are in control for efficient use of resources and effective production of outputs. Step-by-step implementation is achieved through structured project management for which team members are trained. Employees are forced to see themselves and the organisation as their customers see them, and the logic of the marketplace and marketing practice is spread through the organisation. The emphasis is away from control by managers and supervisors and towards self-control. The teams decide *how to* do things, whilst management are concerned with outputs of processes. Managers as resource allocators and decision makers are managed by internal customers and become facilitators of good customer service. All must have both *responsibility* and *authority* for service quality which is enhanced by common purpose and coherence. Strategy formulation and implementation can and should be marketing-led to ensure that organisational change is market-led and efficiently achieved. Sustainable competitive strategy must be well understood by the implementors who have played their part in creating it and have a real desire to change in response to market needs derived from clear customer focus for the benefit of the whole organisation.

Quality is still seen in many organisations as largely about product conformity to specification, and tends to be sited firmly within operations, and therefore true organisation-wide customer-orientation and marketing-orientation are not as prevalent as many writers have urged. Many supplying organisations fail to see that they cannot avoid giving service to their customers, and this applies to both manufacturers and service sector. Many see service quality issues as secondary concerns after productivity and resource allocation problems. Customer satisfaction is still believed to be the (exclusive) domain of the marketer and marketing department, and often is not measured and monitored in any case.

The internal marketing concept can be operationalised to provide a link between the organisation's capability and the market's needs and wants. That is, the organisation can be adaptive to its business environment by adding value in terms which are important to customers. Internal marketing is a strategic weapon which helps to achieve excellent service quality and thereby greater customer satisfaction [George, 1990]. In internal marketing the 'product' is not simply a given plan supplied by managers to their internal customers. The internal marketing mechanism ensures, through internal market research and responsive internal product and service design and delivery (i.e., appropriate resource allocation as part of facilitation), that internal customers (employees) get the resources they need in order to best serve their customers, but only if they are inclined to do so. This two-way communication of needs and wants and feedback on performance measures and satisfaction is the *'learning organisation'* in action:

> "strategy creation is seen as emerging from the way a company, at various levels, acquires, interprets and processes information about its environment" [Pettigrew and Whipp, 1991: 136].

Thus, internal marketing drives a systematic process of environmental analysis by mapping, classifying and analysing environmental variables and communicate conclusions widely. This provides a deep understanding of the total environment rather than relying on the feeling of experienced executives [de Vasconcellos Filho, 1985].

The mechanism conditions the organisation for change, develops a capacity to change, and achieves a critical mass for adoption of a given strategy. But this change-facilitation mechanism should perhaps not be termed 'internal marketing' since that suggests it is the sole domain of marketers. Change management is not to be 'hi-jacked' by marketing specialists and held within the marketing function. Rather, change management and responsiveness to chosen markets (i.e. strategic management) requires marketing principles to be applied throughout an organisation, i.e. the organisation has to develop sensitivity to customer needs and change in technology, customer needs, competitors, etc. This is, of course, the classical argument for a marketing orientation. What is required, further, is a more holistic management approach as a learning organisation. The knowledge base [Pettigrew and Whipp, 1991], beliefs and values are then shared for mutual benefit throughout the organisation by pursuing a single corporate objective of profit from customer satisfaction. The development of the organisational knowledge base is argued for by Pettigrew and Whipp [1991: 178].

The implementation of strategic change should not be attempted as a single pro-gramme. Instead a small series of efforts are worked on with appointed 'change managers' at different levels in the organisation. In parallel, the reward and communications systems are used, often leading to substantial adjustment. With constant monitoring and feedback of the process such mechanisms can generate valuable information which enables management to modify the original inten-tion over time. It does not make sense to treat internal marketing as a specialist functional approach. It really represents the convergence of a number of previ-ously separate management technologies, such as human resource development, employee relations, strategic management, quality management, marketing, etc. It is increasingly recognised that managing a business is an integration of these many functional specialisms, and that management is a continual and complex process and cannot be seen as a sequence of discrete steps. Indeed, as far back as Mintzberg [1973] it has been recognised that the work of the manager is not com-partmentalised into different areas but is a portfolio of skills which are not func-tionally distinguishable and cut across the traditional functions (negotiator, re-source allocator, information disseminator, etc.).

It is proposed that the basic ideas which have led to the proliferation of writing on internal marketing are fundamentally sound. However, it is suggested that in or-der to take into account the real problems of achieving customer orientation, be it through marketing orientation or TQM, there is a need for organisational man-agement to develop generalist skills and competencies based on the application of sound marketing principles throughout the organisation. A form of internal marketing can provide the mechanism for the major re-orientation needed in so many organisations. However, the view that internal marketing is solely the do-main of marketers is too narrow and does not truly take the needs of internal cus-tomers into account. In this respect, the current interpretations of the internal marketing concept are too 'product'-orientated, being based on the traditional marketing concept, rather than marketing-orientated, and marketers must put their own house in order on this matter before they can hope to demonstrate the true worth of the marketing concept as a business management paradigm. Major change programmes and plans clearly present problems and Mastenbroek [1991: 243] has suggested that continual internal and external marketing are more effec-tive in bringing about organisational change. This is supported by Johnson and Scholes [1989: 314] who argue that the consolidation of acceptance of significant change is vital and is achieved through communications:

"...it is the political and cultural barriers to change that may well provide the major stumbling blocks to the implementation of strategic change" [Johnson and Scholes, 1989: 46].

The role of internal marketing in achieving evolutionary or transformational change has been suggested:

"One of the best ways to overcome barriers to plan implementation is to involve many levels and departments in development of the plan. One of the best ways to do this is to conduct internal research using professionals in order to develop a sense of the current mission and to gather the insights and dream agenda of your executives and staff" [Bill Weylock, private communication via Internet, 1992].

Thomson [1990] has identified people issues and organisation issues within the context of the culture of the organisation. The former are concerned with maximising relationships within the organisation where individuals, teams, managers, and leaders are seen as internal 'target' customers with needs which can be satisfied through the generation of internal 'products & services'. The latter includes practices, plans, structure, vision, mission, and values and is concerned with maximising (the utilisation of) resources.

The terminology is yet to develop fully to the point where a single clear understanding of the underlying principles of internal marketing is widespread among managers. Some strong resistance to the use of the term 'internal marketing' has been experienced, as it suggests that the mechanism of change management being described is the exclusive property of marketers. The term *'Internal Relationship Marketing'* is proposed as a development of other terms used by writers discussed. This new term recognises the applicability of the marketing concept through the identification of exchanges of value between the employer and employee and between the organisation and its customers. It also recognises differing goals between the parties to these exchanges, within the overall organisational goal of achieving profitable long-run customer satisfaction and loyalty through demonstrated customer orientation. This is pursued in a planned manner by all organisation members as a means to achieving differentiation of the organisation for the purposes of attaining sustainable competitive advantage. Ulrich [1989] has argued that customer satisfaction is not sufficient and that competitive advantage must be sought in the conscious development of customer commitment, i.e., loyalty and devotion which transcends short-term 'feel good' relationships by building interdependencies, shared values and mutually beneficial strategies.

As yet there is no empirical basis for the required theory of internal marketing as a change management concept, whilst at the same time there is empirical data to show that internal marketing, in various forms, is being practised as a viable response by managers to the real problems of achieving the objectives required by strategic decision-making. Internal marketing cannot be viewed as simply the application of marketing concepts within the organisation, nor is it the use of modified human resource management principles. It is a conceptually separate phenomenon which warrants further investigation. Further, much of the literature disregards the difficulty of the political processes, i.e., differing ideas, beliefs, and values held by managers, supervisors and front-line service providers [Dawson, 1994]. This literature is then too prescriptive and too narrow in trying to apply the marketing concept as it has developed as a response to (external) market relationships [Mudie, 1987 and private communication, 1992]. It is thus a "reform ambition" [Strauss and Corbin, 1990] which motivates a research project by one of the authors.

Significance of Vision and Mission Statements

A more precise definition of the term organisation can be suggested, than is generally used in practice. For an 'organisation' to exist all parts must be well co-ordinated and inter-related to further the organisation's overall objectives. Further, the groups of organisation members must be able to (collectively) respond to both internal and external needs for change. If these properties are absent, there is not an organisation in the true sense. Drucker has spoken of "differences in vision".

Every organisation has a range of interested stakeholders who have particular, and often differing, expectations of the business. The strategist must achieve a balanced set of objectives which meet these expectations. The mission statement aims to spell out the central purpose of the organisation and its business, i.e., why it exists, and to develop shared core values which centre on what senior management believes in and provide an essential character for the organisation. Employees can then have a feeling of belonging and a sense of external goals worth striving for. People are more highly motivated and work more intelligently if they believe in what they are doing and trust their organisation, and this engenders commitment and loyalty. Employees can be inspired by a clear sense of direction and commercial rationale which a statement of strategic intent or vision can provide and this must also identify major policies which define behaviours and standards for how stakeholders should be treated and how the company operates [Campbell and Tawaday, 1990; Doyle, 1994].

Internal marketing has a role to play in developing a common mission and shared vision of where the organisation can and should go in the future, as this must be fit with its capabilities and the opportunities which the environment offers. But this often is not achieved, as according to Wilson *et al.* [1992: 135], the mission statement:

> "has the potential for providing employees with a clear understanding of core corporate values; ... many organisations still lack a mission statement; ... others have statements which reflect a degree of wishful thinking rather than reality...".

Illustrative Cases

Two case studies are now discussed which are based on consultancy assignments carried out by one of the authors. These cases have been chosen to illustrate the powerful effects of internal marketing and to show that without such a programme it is likely that the new strategy of each organisation would have been of little value.

Both organisations developed a strong and focused programme of internal marketing when previously there had been no such initiative. The two organisations can be contrasted due to their differences in size, type of market, types of staffing (one with a professional ethos, the other craft skills), organisational structures, and type of output (one an emotive service, the other a manufactured high-value product).

The Health Care Provider

The British National Health Service (NHS) is currently undergoing some of its biggest changes and challenges since its initial development in the immediate post-war period. These changes, which are being driven by government, are designed to contain costs, improve quality and accountability, and introduce a service which is more responsive to patients' needs. As part of the strategy to achieve this, a series of changes have been made, including the development of self-governing hospital trusts (SGHT) characterised by more overtly professional management structures.

For many of the hospitals faced with this, including the one covered by this consultancy assignment, the nature and significance of the magnitude of the changes demanded has proved to be considerable and has led to a number of major changes in managerial culture. Perhaps the most prominent of these is a shift from what was traditionally been an internal and largely reactive focus to one which has a far stronger external orientation and characterised not just by better day-to-day management, but also by an emphasis upon long-term planning and a heightening of priorities.

In the case of planning, the majority of hospital managers have traditionally had poorly developed few skills, having worked for many years very largely on the basis of annual budgeting. However, faced with the need to reduce waiting times, increase efficiency levels and fight for business from fund-holding general practitioners, the need to develop these skills and highlight areas of competitive advantage has been paramount.

In the case of the client discussed here, an audit of managerial skills led us to classify the managers in terms of two dimensions:

- their effectiveness as day-to-day managers; and
- the quality of their long-term planning skills

This led to the matrix that appears in Figure 5.2 [from Gilligan and Lowe, 1994: 62].

Long-term planning abilities

		Low	High
Day-to-day managerial effectiveness	Low	The bumblers & the dodos who are out of touch and unlikely to survive in the long term 1	The long-sighted strumblers who constantly experience short-term problems 3
	High	The myopics who will stagnate 2	The visionaries who will thrive 4

Figure 5.2 Health Service managers and the short and long-term management skills matrix

However, because the management task within hospitals is also shared with se-nior medical staff, the audit included them and led to the matrix in Figure 5.3 [from Gilligan and Lowe, 1994: 62]. The senior medical staff are all 40-65 years old, have considerable medical consultant skills, are highly regarded within the pro-fession, have responsibilities for a medical directorate (e.g., neurosurgery, obstet-rics, accident & emergency), but have no formal management training. They are now held accountable, with a business manager, for the strategic direction of their directorate and performance levels of staff and now have budget responsibility.

Their ability to manage effectively

		Low	High
Their willingness to manage	Low	the incompetent meddlers 1	the opt-outs & ostriches 3
	High	the dangermedics 2	the supermedics 4

Figure 5.3 Health Service doctors and the short and long-term management skills matrix

In the case both of the managers and the medical staff, the initial audit led to the majority being placed in cell 2, although they were typically perceived by their staff to be almost exclusively in cell 1.

The tasks that we were faced with can be summarised in terms of the need to:

- improve planning skills;
- improve day-to-day managerial skills;
- achieve a greater external focus;
- identify areas of competitive advantage and develop an approach to management and planning which reflected this;
- develop a stronger, clearer and more positive external image;
- develop a sense of vision; and
- communicate these messages to staff internally and involve them in the change process as far as possible.

The most problematic of these was felt to be the final point, since a largely mechanistic and hierarchical approach to management had characterised the hospital previously. As part of the effort to overcome this, a programme of *internal marketing* was developed. This involved detailed discussions with staff within each of the departments and the development of SWOT analyses, the subsequent identification of three areas of distinct and sustainable competitive advantage, a mission statement, a clear set of departmental and corporate objectives, and a detailed action plan which highlighted areas of responsibility and accountability, performance feedback measures and the timescales over which objectives would be achieved.

Considerable attention was paid to the development of far stronger and more open communication patterns and to feeding back information on objectives and progress to staff throughout the hospital. At the same time, a series of quality circles was established.

As with many cases, the initial changes came about only slowly, but with the appointment of a new chief executive for the hospital, an obvious commitment on his part to achieve the culture shifts that were needed, as well as a series of highly publicised successes in developing new business, the programme gained momentum.

The Manufacturer

The company was a well-established and, until shortly before the consultancy assignment, financially successful builder of medium-sized high performance power boats, based on the south coast of England. The company's products have developed a strong reputation for quality and an intensely knowledgeable and loyal customer base.

The company's approach to selling was traditionally reactive, something which had been possible because for many years they had been able to sell everything they had made. However, at the end of the 1980s, demand for the company's products plummeted as sales of expensive luxury items were hit by the recession in the UK. The company responded by cutting prices, although sales failed to respond and continued to decline.

Faced with this, the managing director decided upon a radical new strategy which involved the development of a new and less expensive range of boats which would capitalise upon the company's very strong brand values. One of the authors was called in to advise on the implementation of the new approach.

The implications for the company of the new strategy were significant both in terms of the approaches to manufacturing and to marketing and sales. The new range was to be targeted at a sector of the market which, whilst made up of sailing enthusiasts, was less knowledgeable about boats and sailing than the market sector that the company had traditionally sold to. The implications of this were not only that a new distribution and sales network was needed, but also that a new approach to manufacturing was required in which outputs would be far higher, the attention to cost control far higher as the company shifted from unit production techniques to a semi-production line approach. At the same time, the company would need to fill skills gaps in sales and administration by recruiting new staff. It was recognised also that there would be a major shift in patterns of work, with several members of the workforce having to develop new areas of expertise and work to far tighter timetables.

The consultancy assignment consisted of two arms: the first involved the formulation of the new marketing and sales strategy, whilst the second focused upon a programme of *internal marketing*. In the case of the internal programme, the primary objective was seen to be that of ensuring that levels of motivation, commitment and morale remained high. The majority of the workforce of forty had been with the company for a considerable time and a strong sense of family and craft values prevailed. It was perhaps because of this, and the low key and informal managerial style that prevailed, as well as the way in which the sacrifices that were being made by the managing director and his family were highly visible (the sale of some property with the proceeds being ploughed back into the company, the disposal of a company car, and a 50% cut in the MD's salary) that the task of *internal marketing* proved to be relatively easy.

The company was characterised by very open and informal patterns of communication. From the outset, the employees had been kept fully informed by the managing director of the magnitude of the problems facing the company and were aware that either there would be a need for redundancies or major changes in working practice. The introduction of the new range of boats was therefore seen by the workforce to be the far preferable alternative, even though it involved a series of major changes in working practice.

The launch of the new range in 1990 proved to be a success and was reinforced by better than forecast sales in the 1991-93 sailing seasons. It was perhaps because of this and the consequent security of employment that the programme of internal marketing proved to be equally successful with levels of morale and motivation remaining high.

Conclusions

Our examination of the growing body of knowledge on the nature and role of internal marketing [Varey, 1995a and 1995b] has been illuminated by the application of the approach in two very different organisations operating in very different and changing environments. This has led us to conclude that:

Internal marketing is a process and mechanism for ensuring effective responsiveness to environmental changes, flexibility for adopting newly designed organisational arrangements efficiently, and continuous improvement in performance. Internal marketing can assist the organisation to match its responses to environmental change and to continuously enhance its capability.

Some observations can be made on a suitable approach for operating the internal marketing concept as a programme for positive change in organisational arrangements. The organisation must have a measure of how well it is meeting the demands of its environment. Personal contact is the preferred method for customer satisfaction research to provide a benchmark for how well service quality is perceived by customers as a starting point for managing for change. Employee interviews, focus groups and surveys are then required to assess the internal service culture of the organisation and to identify target groups for the promotion of the marketing concept. Internal customer groups can then be segmented by level of customer contact. Internal communications can then be tailored for each group to reinforce service quality and must be used in specifying what is expected of them by stating specific measurable behaviours. Rewards for all must be based on measured personal internal service quality goals, and recognition of good service quality role models must be given via a variety of internal communications channels and external media such as advertising to acknowledge outstanding service.

Employees are encouraged to communicate with customers by being freed from routine tasks, whilst personal development and training is centred on service quality competences and, by using performance data collected, aims to challenge assumptions about the customer's role and requirements. There must be a clear focus on building supportive working relationships, which might be termed 'intimate co-operation', to break down and cross barriers between departments, based on trust through good communication and realistic promises kept, rather than only on external customer transactions. This requires development and articulation of mutual expectations.

A framework of concepts and skills must be developed and used to deliberately and systematically improve the processes of the organisation which impact on service outputs and thereby service quality perceptions of customers. Specifically there must be a clear perspective on what the organisation is trying to achieve and the contribution that is expected of staff. Clear and strong lines of communication, positive feedback and clear personal and organisational values are vital aspects of effective internal marketing.

References

Barney, J.B., 1986, 'Organisational Culture: Can It Be a Source of Sustained Competitive Advantage?', *Academy of Management Review*, 11 (3), pp.656-665.

Beer, M., Eisenstat, R.A. and Spector, B., 1990, 'Why Change Programmes Don't Produce Change', *Harvard Business Review*, Nov.-Dec., pp.158-166.

Berry, L.L., Zeithaml, V.A. and Parasuraman, A., 1990, 'Five Imperatives for Improving Service Quality', *Sloan Management Review*, Summer, pp.29-38.

Brown, R., 1993, *Market Focus: Achieving and Sustaining Marketing Effectiveness*, Oxford: Butterworth-Heinemann.

Burns, T. and Stalker, R., 1961, *The Management of Innovation*, London: Tavistock.

Campbell, A. and Tawaday, K., 1990, *Mission & Business Philosophy: Winning Employee Commitment*, Oxford: Heinemann Professional.

Chaudhry-Lawton, R., Lawton, R., Murphy, K. and Terry, A., 1992, *Quality: Change Through Teamwork*, Century Books.

Checkland, P.B. and Scholes, J., 1990, *Soft Systems Methodology in Action*, Chichester: John Wiley.

Davidson, H., 1987, *Offensive Marketing*, 2nd Edition, Harmondsworth: Penguin Business.

Dawson, P., 1994, *Organisational Change: A Processual Approach*, London: Paul Chapman Publishing.

de Vasconcellos Filho, P., 1985, 'Environmental Analysis for Strategic Planning', *Managerial Planning*, 33 (4).

Donaldson, L., 1987, 'Strategy, Structural Adjustment to Regain Fit and Performance: In Defence of Contingency Theory', *Journal of Management Studies*, 24 (2), pp.1-24.

Doyle, P., 1994, *Marketing Management & Strategy*, Hemel Hempstead: Prentice-Hall International.

George, W.R., 1990, 'Internal Marketing and Organisational Behaviour: A Partnership in Developing Customer-Conscious Employees at Every Level', *Journal of Business Research*, 20, pp.63-70.

Gilligan, C.T. and Lowe, R., 1994, *Marketing and General Practice*, Radcliffe Press.

Gummesson, E., 1987, 'The New Marketing - Developing Long-Term Interactive Relationships', *Long Range Planning*, 20 (4), pp.10-20.

Handy, C., 1989, *The Age of Unreason*, Arrow Books.

Handy, C., 1994, *The Empty Raincoat: Making Sense of the Future*, Hutchinson.

Heskett, J.L., 1992, 'A Service Sector Paradigm for Management: The Service Sector Profit Chain', *Proceedings of the Service Sector Management Research Workshop*, Cranfield School of Management.

Johnson, G. and Scholes, K., 1989, *Exploring Corporate Stratgey — Text and Cases*, 2nd edition, Hemel-Hempstead: Prentice-Hall International.

Lawton, R.L., 1991, 'Creating a Customer-Centred Culture in Service Industries', *Quality Progress*, September, pp.69-72.

Mastenbroek, W.F.G., ed.), 1991, *Managing for Quality in the Service Sector*, Oxford: Blackwell.

Mintzberg, H., 1973, *The Nature of Managerial Work*, New York: Harper & Row.

Möller, K. and Anttila, M., 1987, 'Marketing Capability — A Key Success Factor for Small Business?', *Journal of Marketing Management*, 3 (2), pp.185-203.

Mudie, P., 1987, 'Internal Marketing: Cause for Concern', *Quarterly Review of Marketing*, Spring/Summer, pp.21-24.

Parasuraman, A., Zeithaml, V.A. and Berry, L.L., 1988, 'SERVQUAL: A Multiple-Item Scale for Measuring Consumer Perceptions of Service Quality', *Journal of Retailing*, 64 (1), pp.12-40.

Payne, A.F., 1988, 'Developing a Marketing-Oriented Organisation', *Business Horizons*, May-June, pp.46-53.

Peters, T., 1992, *Liberation Management*, Macmillan.

Pettigrew, A. and Whipp, R., 1991, *Managing Change for Competitive Success*, Oxford: Blackwell Business Books.

Pugh, D.S. , Hickson, D.J. and Hinings, C R., 1971, *Writers on Organisations*, London: Penguin.

Quinn, M. and Humble, J., 1993, 'Using Service to Gain a Competitive Edge — The PROMPT Approach', *Long Range Planning*, 26 (2), pp.31-40.

Sharp, B., 1991, 'Marketing Orientation: More Than Just Customer Focus', *International Marketing Review*, 8 (4), pp.20-25.

Strauss, A. and Corbin, J., 1990, *Basics of Qualitative Research*, London: Sage Publications.

Thomson, K., 1990, *The Employee Revolution - The Rise of Corporate Internal Marketing*, London: Pitman Publishing.

Tjosvold, D., 1992, *Team Organisation: An Enduring Competitive Advantage*, John Wiley.

Ulrich, D., 1989, 'Tie the Corporate Knot: Gaining Complete Customer Commitment', *Sloan Management Review*, Summer, pp.19-27.

Vail, P.B., 1989, *Managing as a Performing Art*, San Francisco: Jossey-Bass.

Van de Ven, A., 1986, 'Central Problems in the Management of Innovation', *Management Science*, 32 (5), pp.590-607.

Varey, R.J., 1995a, 'Internal Marketing: A Review and Some Inter-Disciplinary Research Challenges', *International Journal of Service Industry Management*, 6 (1).

Varey, R.J., 1995b, 'A Model of Internal Marketing for Building and Sustaining a Competitive Service Advantage', in forthcoming special issue, *Journal of Marketing Management*.

Wellins, R., Byham, W. and Wilson, J., 1991, *Empowering Teams*, San Francisco: Jossey-Bass.

Wilson, R.M.S. and Gilligan, C.T. with Pearson, D.J., 1992, *Strategic Marketing Management: Planning, implementation and control*, Oxford: Butterworth-Heinemann.

Witcher, B., 1990, 'The Role of Total Quality Management in the Creation of Market Responsive Organisation', Occasional Paper No 9173, Durham University Business School.

6

Measurement of Service Quality: The Effect of Contextuality

Michèle Paulin[1] and Jean Perrien[2]

SERVQUAL, a measurement tool well known in the service quality research literature, has been more academic than managerial. It is postulated that SERVQUAL measurement errors are to a large extent due to contextual factors. In fact, contextuality is a major epistemological issue in social sciences. Contextual factors are related to the units of study (U), the study observations (O) and the type of study (T). A content analysis of SERVQUAL studies on their U-O-T, reveals that a universal scale may not provide adequate answers to the management and measurement of service quality.

Introduction

Much of the success of Japanese firms since World War II has been attributed to their management of quality [Crosby, 1979, 1984, 1989; Deming, 1960, 1988; Feigenbaum, 1961, 1985; Ishikawa, 1985, 1990; Juran, 1982, 1987a, 1987b, 1992; Juran and Gryna, 1980]. The post-industrial economy of today is characterised by a growing importance of the services sector. In addition, the service component is recognised as a significant means of added-value for manufactured goods. Therefore, the concept of service quality has recently received considerable academic and managerial interest [Bell and Zemke, 1991; Berry and Parasuraman, 1991; Berry, Bennett and Brown, 1989; Garvin, 1988; Grönroos, 1984, 1988, 1990a, 1990b; Gummesson and Grönroos, 1987; Haywood-Farmer and Nollet, 1991; Juran, 1992; Knisely, 1979; Normann, 1991; Zeithaml, Parasuraman and Berry, 1990]. However, from a managerial point of view, a concept such as service quality must be meaningful, able to be operationalised and measurable [Garvin, 1988]. Parasuraman, Zeithaml and Berry [1985, 1986, 1988, 1994], Parasuraman, Berry and Zeithaml [1991] and Zeithaml, Berry and Parasuraman [1993] developed the well-known SERVQUAL scale as an instrument for measuring service quality. This scale has been subjected to a

1   Michèle Paulin, L.L.B., M.B.A., is a doctoral student in Services Marketing and International Business, Université du Québec à Montréal, Canada.
2   Jean Perrien, Ph.D. is Professor at the Marketing Department, Université du Québec à Montréal.

great number of analyses and has received critical attention in the research literature.

The purpose of this paper is to examine the SERVQUAL literature from the perspective of contextuality. It is not our intention to do a meta-analysis or to include all the studies on SERVQUAL. Based on a framework suggested by Cronbach [1986], it is postulated that conflicting interpretations in the SERVQUAL literature, particularly in regards to its validity, may be due to contextuality and that one cannot effectively assess this measurement tool without considering or controlling for these contextual factors.

SERVQUAL: Conceptual Foundations

The complexity of the quality concept has been pointed out by Garvin [1988]. He describes five definitions of quality: (i) transcendental, (ii) product-based, (iii) value-based, (iv) manufacturing-based, and (v) user-based. In the following paragraphs, the conceptual foundations of the quality concept and its measurement are explored taking into consideration these five definitions.

Transcendental quality is a subjective judgement made by the producer. For instance, an artist will assess the quality of his or her production on the basis of internal criteria. This is a common pattern in the artistic world. 'Schools' (for example, hyper-realism, cubism, ...) define the internal dimensions of this judgement of quality.

Product-based quality focuses on the ingredients or attributes as well as the costs associated with the product's components. The perception of quality is proportional to the perceived value of these components.

Value-based quality is a relativistic view of quality. For instance, both a Honda Civic and a Mercedes may be perceived as being high-quality products when taking into account their respective prices.

Manufacturing-based quality is related to the production process. In this case, quality is measured on the basis of internal norms of design or specifications as defined by the producer. Quality control is a major concern for both manufacturing and service firms [Deming, 1960; Feigenbaum, 1961, 1985; Ishikawa, 1985, 1990]. The objective is to reduce the costs due to production and service delivery errors and dissatisfied customers [Crosby, 1979, 1984, 1989; Deming, 1988; Garvin, 1988; Juran, 1982, 1987a, 1987b, 1992; Juran and Gryna, 1980].

User-based quality is a global assessment by the client. This definition would incorporate Oliver's [1977, 1980] 'disconfirmation paradigm' and Grönroos' [1984] concept of perceived quality as being a judgement of the difference between the customer's expectations for a product or service versus the actual experiencing of the product or service. Customer's expectations are based on their needs as well as the information they are exposed to. With regard to services, user-based quality also involves judgements of the technical and functional aspects of service delivery. The former focuses on the core of the offering or 'what' the client receives, whereas the latter relates to 'how' the service is delivered [Grönroos, 1984].

Two managerial approaches to service quality [Grönroos, 1984, Parasuraman *et al.*, 1985] have integrated both user and manufacturing-based definitions of quality.

The 'service product' approach of Grönroos [1990a] considers service quality as a possible competitive advantage for a firm and, thus, is strategic in nature. Within this approach, manufacturing-based quality stresses quality control on the design, the production and the delivery of the service. Concomitantly, the concept of user-based quality also permeates the 'service product' approach since present and future client needs are considered in planning, implementing and evaluating the service.

Parasuraman *et al.* [1985, 1986, 1988] and Zeithaml *et al.* [1990] developed an approach to service quality management based on the analyses of deficiencies identified as service quality 'gaps'. The principal gap involves the difference between customer expectations and perceptions of the actual performance in the delivery of a service. This is clearly user-based quality assessment and is similar to that described by Grönroos [1984]. In addition, the 'gap' approach hypothesises that this user-based gap is caused by a set of four organisational gaps, two of which relate to manufacturing-based quality. First, the translation of customers expectations into performance specifications and, second, the adherence to those specifications during the actual delivery of the service. The other two gaps describe deficiencies in information about customer expectations and in communications describing the firm's service to customers.

Development of SERVQUAL

Parasuraman *et al.* [1985, 1986, 1988] and Zeithaml *et al.* [1990] conducted a series of empirical studies to determine the underlying dimensions used by customers when assessing service quality. A first survey, conducted by a consulting firm, focused on the services of retail banking, credit card companies, long-distance telephone, real estate brokers, and domestic appliance repair and maintenance. A set of 97 paired questions, expectations and perceptions of service quality was analysed using multivariate analysis. The resulting ten dimensions of service quality were: tangibles, reliability, responsiveness, communication, credibility, security, competence, courtesy, understanding/knowing customers and access. With subsequent studies and analyses, SERVQUAL was then reduced to 22 pairs of questions giving rise to five dimensions. These were: tangibles, reliability, responsiveness, assurance and empathy [Parasuraman *et al.*, 1986, 1988; Zeithaml *et al.*, 1990].

Reliability of SERVQUAL

Using Cronbach's measure of internal consistency, several analyses revealed that the scale depicts some overall reliability when used in a variety of service industry contexts (see Table 6.1). There is, however, some variance among studies when looking at individual service quality dimensions. For instance, the alpha coefficient varies from 0.50 to 0.87 on the empathy dimension and from 0.52 to 0.82 for tangibles.

Validity of SERVQUAL

Content as well as construct validities of SERVQUAL have been assessed by Parasuraman *et al.* [1986; 1988]. Using the multi-traits, multi-methods matrix, they investigated both the nomological and trait validities of the construct. Their results, using both expectations and perceptions of customers, confirmed the relevance of their scale, as far as validity was concerned. Nomological validity was estimated by correlating measures of quality with two judgement-based measures of customers' perceptions. Trait validity was assessed by correlating the five dimensions of the construct. The average correlation between dimensions was fairly low (range from 0.21 for banking services to 0.26 for maintenance services).

Table 6.1 Reliability of SERVQUAL

STUDY	CRONBACH ALPHA	STUDY	CRONBACH ALPHA
Babakus and Mangold [1992]	Expectations: Reliability: 0.68 Responsiveness: 0.72 Assurance: 0.80 Empathy: 0.50 Tangibles: 0.59 Perceptions: Reliability: 0.76 Responsiveness: 0.90 Assurance: 0.89 Empathy: 0.87 Tangibles: 0.78	Freeman and Dart [1993]	Tangibles: 0.65 Timeliness: 0.74 Assurance: 0.72 Fee-related: 0.75 Professionalism: 0.71 Empathy: 0.64 Exceptional Situations: 0.56 Overall scale: 0.79
Carman [1990]	Mean alpha 0.75 for 35 scales retained	Lapierre [1993]	Perceptions: Technical reliability: 0.86 Functional implications: 0.91 Technical competence: 0.84 Functional reliability: 0.84 Functional accessibility: 0.57 Functional courtesy: 0.84 Functional continuity: 0.54 0n 41 items: 0.97
Cronin and Taylor [1992]	Banking: 0.89 Exterminator: 0.90 Dry cleaning: 0.90 Fast Food: 0.85	Lévesque and Mc-Dougall [1992]	Expectations: Reliability: 0.82 Responsiveness: 0.71 Assurance: 0.59 Empathy: 0.81 Tangibles: 0.82 Perceptions: Reliability: 0.89 Responsiveness: 0.89 Assurance: 0.90 Empathy: 0.86 Tangibles: 0.71 SERVQUAL: Reliability: 0.88 Responsiveness: 0.85 Assurance: 0.84 Empathy: 0.84 Tangibles: 0.70

Table 1 (continued): Reliability of SERVQUAL

STUDY	CRONBACH ALPHA	STUDY	CRONBACH ALPHA
Csipak [1991]	Expectations: 0.88 Reliability: 0.69 Responsiveness: 0.63 Assurance: 0.71 Empathy: 0.58 Tangibles: 0.73 Perceptions: 0.96 Reliability: 0.89 Responsiveness: 0.86 Assurance: 0.91 Empathy: 0.87 Tangibles: 0.78 SERVQUAL overall scale: 0.94 Reliability: 0.84 Responsiveness: 0.74 Assurance: 0.86 Empathy: 0.75 Tangibles: 0.67	Parasuraman *et al.* [1988]	(2nd scale purification of SERVQUAL) Bank: Reliability: 0.80 Responsiveness: 0.72 Assurance: 0.84 Empathy: 0.71 Tangibles: 0.52 Credit card company: Reliability: 0.78 Responsiveness: 0.69 Assurance: 0.80 Empathy: 0.80 Tangibles: 0.62 Repair and Maintenance Company: Reliability: 0.84 Responsiveness: 0.76 Assurance: 0.87 Empathy: 0.72 Tangibles: 0.64 Long-Distance Telephone Company: Reliability: 0.74 Responsiveness: 0.70 Assurance: 0.84 Empathy: 0.76 Tangibles: 0.64
Finn and Lamb [1991]	Variation of 0.59 (tangibles) to 0.83 (reliability) for percep- tions	Reidenbach and San- difer-Smallwood [1990]	Patient confidence: 0.95 Business competence: 0.86 Quality of the treatment: 0.80 Support services: 0.80 Physical appearance: 0.75 Waiting time: 0.83 Empathy: 0.84

Contextuality and SERVQUAL Investigations

In a provocative, albeit stimulating paper, Cronbach [1986] points out that conflict-ing results in social sciences research may be due to contextual factors which are intrinsic features of any empirical investigation. To understand contextuality, Cronbach suggests using a framework for classifying factors related to three aspects of any empirical investigation: the units of study (U), i.e., the respondents; the ob-servations (O), which describe the study's measurements and the methods of data collection, and the treatment (T), which refers to the purpose of the investigation. Hence, any empirical investigation in social sciences may be analysed in terms of UOT.

This article exposes the contextuality of several empirical studies using the SERVQUAL scale. Indeed, several investigators have challenged the relevance of this scale [Boulding, Kalra, Staelin and Zeithaml, 1993; Brown, Churchill and Peter, 1993; Cronin and Taylor, 1992, 1994; Parasuraman *et al.*, 1991, 1994; Zeithaml *et al.*, 1993; Teas, 1993, 1994]. However, none of these criticisms included a contextual analysis of the major factors contributing to variance among the SERVQUAL investigations. For instance, how can one compare the results of service quality measurement in health care services with those in the transportation industry without taking into account the nature of the respective customers (U), the manner in which the customers are questioned about the services (O) and the purpose of the services involved (T)?

The Units of Study 'U'

Contextual factors related to the units of a study (U) include: the type of respondent, the type of services used, the sampling methods for selecting the respondents, the sample size and the response rate from the sample (see Table 6.2). Only a few SERVQUAL studies [Csipak, 1991; Freeman and Dart, 1993; Lapierre, 1993; Lévesque and McDougall, 1992; Mangold and Babakus, 1991] adequately describe the profile of the type of respondents surveyed. This is all the more surprising given the importance of segmentation as a marketing concept. Segmentation forces the firm to identify the pertinent characteristics of the targeted clientele. In this case, these characteristics might well influence the assessment of service quality from the external client perspective.

More interestingly, two studies investigated the type of respondent in terms of internal and external clients. Mangold and Babakus [1991] observed differences in the perception of service quality among patients, managers and employees of an hospital, whereas Saleh and Ryan [1991] drew a comparison of service quality assessments between the administrative staff and clients of an hotel. However, these studies did not evaluate the underlying methodological problem of whether these different types of respondents use different criteria for judging service quality.

In the vast majority of SERVQUAL studies, the type of respondent is only described in terms of the sector of the service industry: patients [Babakus and Mangold, 1992; Mangold and Babakus, 1991; Peyrot, Cooper and Schnapf, 1993; Reidenbach and Sandifer-Smallwood, 1990], students [Carman, 1990; Fick and Ritchie, 1991; Lévesque and McDougall, 1992], consumers [Carman, 1990; Cronin and Taylor, 1992; Csipak, 1991; Finn and Lamb, 1991; Parasuraman *et al.*, 1988, 1991], hotel clients [Saleh and Ryan, 1991], industrial services buyers in the chemical industry [Keirl and Mitchell, 1990], consultant engineers [Lapierre, 1993] and accounting and financial services [Bojanic, 1991; Freeman and Dart, 1993; Morgan, 1990].

The uniqueness of each type of service is dependent on the service sector, the competitive structure of particular markets, the characteristics of the macro-environment and the customer's buying processes. SERVQUAL studies have differed considerably with respect to the service sector surveyed (see Table 6.2). In general, four groups of services have been investigated: (1) health care services [Babakus and Mangold, 1992; Mangold and Babakus, 1991; Peyrot *et al.*, 1993; Reidenbach and Sandifer-Smallwood, 1990]; (2) tourism [Csipak, 1991; Fick and Ritchie, 1991; Saleh and Ryan, 1991]; (3) consumer services [Carman, 1990; Cronin and Taylor, 1992; Lévesque and McDougall, 1992; Parasuraman *et al.*, 1988, 1991], and (4) industrial services [Bojanic, 1991; Freeman and Dart, 1993; Keirl and Mitchell, 1990; Lapierre, 1993; Morgan, 1990]. In some studies, several types of services were assessed [Carman, 1990; Cronin and Taylor, 1992; Fick and Ritchie, 1991; Parasuraman *et al.*, 1988, 1991; Reidenbach and Sandifer-Smallwood, 1990].

SERVQUAL investigations on health care services have dealt with the competitive American environment. One should question the appropriateness of generalizing these findings to state-run medicare system in Canada or to the European environment. Similarly, the deregulation in the British legal system has resulted in a more competitive environment where law firms are obliged to better serve their corporate clients than in the past [Morgan, 1990]. The real possibility that customer assessment of quality in a given service sector would change over time can also be illustrated by the effect of deregulation in the 1980s in the North American commercial banking industry. This deregulation has resulted in a shift from transactional to relational marketing strategies whereby closer and more long-term ties are developed with the customer [Perrien, Filiatrault and Ricard, 1993].

The SERVQUAL studies in the tourist sector were conducted in Canada and the type of service varied significantly. For instance, Fick and Ritchie [1991], evaluated four different types of tourist services as well as banking, Csipak [1991] focused on airplane ticketing and Saleh and Ryan [1991] investigated hotel services. The five studies on retail services investigated retail banking in different times and geographical environments [Carman, 1990; Cronin and Taylor, 1992; Fick and Ritchie, 1991; Lévesque and McDougall, 1992; Parasuraman *et al.*, 1988, 1991].

The customer's buying behaviour has not been adequately controlled for, or considered, as an important contextual factor linked to the type of service. One would hypothesise that the degree of emotional involvement of the respondent with the service would affect the judgement of quality. For instance, one may expect that fast food and dry cleaning [Cronin and Taylor, 1992] would not entail the same level of emotional involvement on the part of the respondent as would health care services [Babakus and Mangold, 1992; Carman, 1990; Mangold and Babakus, 1991; Peyrot *et al.*, 1993].

Variations in sampling methods, size and response rates represent important contextual factors in SERVQUAL studies. Only a few investigations relied on a probabilistic sample [Babakus and Mangold, 1992; Cronin and Taylor, 1992; Mangold and Babakus, 1991; Parasuraman *et al.* 1991; Peyrot *et al.* 1993]. Most of the sampling in SERVQUAL studies was non-probabilistic and to be more precise, was convenience sampling [Bojanic, 1991; Csipak, 1991; Freeman and Dart, 1993; Keirl and Mitchell, 1990; Lapierre, 1993; Lévesque and McDougall, 1992]. Other studies used quota samples [Carman, 1990; Fick and Ritchie, 1991; Finn and Lamb, 1991; Parasuraman *et al.* 1988].

Table 6.2: Units of study 'U'

STUDY *SERVICE SECTOR*	TYPE OF RESPONDENT	TYPE OF SERVICE	SAMPLING METHOD	SAMPLE SIZE (N) RESPONSE RATE (%)
Babakus and Mangold [1992] *Health care services*	Patients	Hospital services	Total population	n=443/1,999 (22 %)
Bojanic [1991] *Professional services*	Small firms of professional services	Corporate accounting	non-probabilistic Convenience sample	n=32/130 (25 %)
Carman [1990] *Consumer services*	Patients, students, consumers	Dental school patient clinic Business school placement centre Tire store Acute care hospital	non-probabilistic Quotas	n=756 Placement centre (n=82) Store (n=74) Others (n>600)
Csipak [1991] *Tourism services*	Travellers using airline as a means of personal transportation	Airline Ticket service	non-probabilistic Convenience sample	n=560 Airline ticket service users (n=280) Travel agency service users (n=280)
Cronin and Taylor [1992] *Consumer services*	Consumers	Extermination Dry cleaning Fast food Banking services	Probabilistic Simple random sampling	n=600
Fick and Ritchie [1991] *Tourism services*	Students	Airlines Hotels Restaurants Ski areas	Non-probabilistic Quotas	n=800
Finn and Lamb [1991] *Consumer services*	Women shoppers	Retailers: K-Mart, Sears, Dillards, Neimann Marcus	Probabilistic Simple random sampling from a commercial list	n=258 Type K-Mart (n=65) " Sears (n=66) " Dillards (n=58) " Neimann Marcus (n=69) (31.9 %)
Freeman and Dart [1993] *Professional services*	Owners and Executives	Corporate accounting	Non-probabilistic Convenience sample	n=217/550 (41 %)
Keirl and Mitchell [1990] *Industrial purchasing services*	Senior buyers of chemical products	Industrial product purchasing	Non-probabilistic Convenience sample	n=88
Lapierre [1993] *Professional services*	Company project manager (clients) by: . activity sector . company size . industry segment	Engineering consulting services	Non-probabilistic Convenience and snow ball sample	n=310/606 project managers
Lévesque and McDougall [1992] *Consumer services*	MBA students and spouses	Main financial institution	Non-probabilistic Convenience sample	n=88

Table 6.2 (continued): Units of study 'U'

STUDY SERVICE SECTOR	TYPE OF RESPONDENT	TYPE OF SERVICE	SAMPLING METHOD	SAMPLE SIZE (N) RESPONSE RATE (%)
Mangold and Babakus [1991] *Health care services*	Patients Employees Managers	Hospital services	Total population	n=443/1,999 patients (22 %) n=110 (employees and managers): n=22 managers n=85 employees n=3 not mention (38 %)
Morgan [1990] *Professional services*	General managers (< 200 employees) Finance director (200 to 500 employees) Company secretary (> 500 employees)	Corporate legal services	Probabilistic Stratified by company size	n=152/600 corporate clients n=42 (<200 employees) n=50 (200 to 500) n=59 (>500 employees)
Parasuraman *et al.* [1988] *Consumer services*	Adult respondents (25 years of age or older equally divided between male and female) recruited by a marketing research firm in a shopping mall	First study: . appliance repair and maintenance . retail banking . long-distance telephone . securities brokerage . credit cards Second study: four nationally known firms: a bank, a credit-card company, a firm offering appliance repair and maintenance services, and a long-distance telephone company	First study: Non-probabilistic For each service a quota of 40 recent users of the service Second study: Non-probabilistic Quotas	First study: n=200 (n=40 by type of services) Second study: n=200 divided equally among companies
Parasuraman *et al.* [1991] *Consumer services*	Clients Contact employees Managers	Telephone company Two insurance companies Two banks	Probabilistic Simple random from 89 unit locations consisting of telephone repair service districts, branch banks, and field offices of insurance companies provided samples of customers, contact employees and managers	n=1,936 clients (21%) n=728 employees (38%) n=231 managers (62%)
Peyrot *et al.* [1993] *Hospital care services*	Outpatients from a free-standing diagnostic imaging facility	Medical clinic	Total population	n=1,366/2,200 (60%)

Table 6.2 (continued): Units of study 'U'

STUDY SERVICE SECTOR	TYPE OF RESPONDENT	TYPE OF SERVICE	SAMPLING METHOD	SAMPLE SIZE (N) RESPONSE RATE (%)
Reidenbach and Sandifer-Smallwood [1990] *Hospital care services*	Users of hospital services	Emergency room Outpatient services Inpatient services	Probabilistic Stratified by services	n=300 emergency (n=50) outpatient (n=190) inpatient (n=60) (73% first call)
Saleh and Ryan [1991] *Tourism services*	Guests staying at a four-star hotel Management staff	Hotel services	Probabilistic Stratified by clients Non-probabilistic for management staff Convenience sample	n=200 clients (85%) n=17 employees

Probabilistic sampling is usually preferred for the purposes of determining external validity. Comparing results from convenience and probabilistic samples is tenuous. However, convenience samples tend to be more homogeneous (e.g., students) than probabilistic samples with respect to the sample size and response rates. Sample size in SERVQUAL studies varies from n=32 [Bojanic, 1991] to n=1366 [Peyrot *et al.* 1993]. It is important to note that sample size has some direct consequences for both the probabilistic error term and the significance of inference tests. No doubt that discrepancies in these two methodological concerns may limit the potential for comparing results of surveys relying on very different sample sizes.

The ability to generalise from the results of a given study also depends on the response rate. Response rates vary drastically among the SERVQUAL surveys: from 22% [Babakus and Mangold, 1992; Mangold and Babakus, 1991] to 85% [Saleh and Ryan, 1991]. Of particular importance in terms of sampling bias is the fact that only one survey explored the characteristics of the non-respondents and the possible consequences of non-responses on the study's results and interpretations [Csipak, 1991].

The Study Observations 'O'

Contextual factors related to a study's observations involve variations of how, when, where, and what data were collected (see Table 6.3). Marketing Research textbooks emphasise that the data-collection method has some direct consequences, not only for the response rate, but also for the accuracy of the data collected (i.e., measurement error). In most SERVQUAL studies, data collection was done by questionnaire, either mailed to the consumer [Babakus and Mangold, 1992; Mangold and Babakus, 1991; Morgan, 1990; Peyrot *et al.*, 1993], or self-administered [Carman, 1990; Lévesque and McDougall, 1992]. Predictably, surveys using mailed questionnaires generated the lowest response rates (see Table 6.2). Only a limited number of surveys were conducted by phone where interaction with the respondent is low [Finn and Lamb, 1991; Reidenbach and Sandifer-Smallwood, 1990]. Several studies used personal interviews [Cronin and Taylor, 1992; Keirl and Mitchell, 1990; Lapierre, 1993; Saleh and Ryan, 1991] which are known to result in a higher level of interaction with the respondents and are often used in quality assessments.

Cronbach [1986] emphasises the importance of time as a contextual factor. The elapsed time between an experience and its measurement is a source of measurement error [Cannel, Oksenberg and Converse, 1977]. The time differential of concern here is the period between the last experience with a service and the time of responding to the SERVQUAL scale. Carman [1990] conducted his research prior to, or just after, the customer's experience. Cronin and Taylor [1992] selected respondents who experienced the service in the past month, whereas Parasuraman *et al.* [1988] relied on respondents who experienced the service in the past three months. Finally, in surveys conducted on health care services, the elapsed time was up to one year [Babakus and Mangold, 1992; Mangold and Babakus, 1991; Reidenbach and Sandifer-Smallwood, 1990].

Another source of variation among studies on how the data was collected is the use of Cronbach's alpha coefficient. This coefficient was not measured or reported in the same way throughout the various studies of SERVQUAL reliability (see Table 6.1). Indeed, the reliability results are reported by computing differences between the responses to the questions on expectations and perceptions [Csipak, 1991; Lévesque and McDougall, 1992; Parasuraman *et al.*, 1991] or by calculating the alpha coefficients separately for expectations and perceptions [Babakus and Mangold, 1992; Csipak, 1991; Lévesque and McDougall, 1992] or by using only the questions on perceptions [Carman, 1990; Lapierre, 1993]. Finally, Cronin and Taylor [1992] only report their findings in terms of the type of service.

In addition, some studies employed the original ten SERVQUAL dimensions without modification [Carman, 1990; Lapierre, 1993]. Others used the five dimensions as reduced by Parasuraman *et al.* [1988] [Csipak, 1991; Finn and Lamb, 1991; Lévesque and McDougall, 1992] or used the five dimensions with modifications [Babakus and Mangold, 1992; Bojanic, 1991; Cronin and Taylor, 1992; Fick and Ritchie, 1991; Freeman and Dart, 1993; Mangold and Babakus, 1991; Morgan, 1990; Saleh and Ryan, 1991]. Finally, Cronin and Taylor [1992], Keirl and Mitchell [1990], Peyrot *et al.* [1993] and Reidenbach and Sandifer-Smallwood [1990] made fundamental modifications to the meaning of the SERVQUAL dimensions.

Not surprisingly, considerable variation among SERVQUAL studies was found for the number of questions and for the type of scale employed. The number of statements ranges from 9 to 97 and they were not always paired statements. A Likert scale was most frequently used and the number of points varied from four, five, seven, or nine. Others used semantic differential, bi-polar or nominal scales.

Table 6.3 Study observations 'O'

Authors	Type of data collection	Service experienced (elapsed time between service and data collection)	Study location	SERVQUAL (dimensions)	Measure
Babakus and Mangold [1992]	Mailed questionnaire No follow up	Patients discharged from hospital within the period of 13 months	Southern U.S.A.	Modified SERVQUAL (5)	15 paired statements (expectations and perceptions) 5-point Likert scale
Bojanic [1991]	Mailed questionnaire No follow up	-	U.S.A.	Modified SERVQUAL (5)	12 statements 5-point Likert scale
Carman [1990]	Written questionnaire completed on site	Before service was received for student placement centre After service was received for other services	California, U.S.A.	Original SERVQUAL (10)	22 statements modified on perceptions for all services except student placement 22 paired statements for student placement centre (expectations and perceptions) 7-point Likert scale
Cronin and Taylor [1992]	Interviews with local residents	Users within the last 30 days Summer of 1988	South-East U.S.A.	Modified SERVQUAL (5)	22 paired statements on expectations and performance 22 statements on importance Statements on consumer satisfaction and purchase intention 7-point Semantic differential
Csipak [1991]	Written questionnaire	Most recent purchase	Montreal Canada	SERVQUAL (5)	22 paired statements (expectations and perceptions) 9-point Likert scale
Fick and Ritchie [1991]	Written questionnaire	Most recent utilisation	Canada	Modified SERVQUAL (5)	33 paired statements (expectations and perceptions) 5-point Likert scale
Finn and Lamb [1991]	Telephone survey	-	Texas, U.S.A.	SERVQUAL (5)	22 paired statements (expectations and perceptions) 5-point Likert scale
Freeman and Dart [1993]	Two mailings of written questionnaire Personal interviews	-	West-Canadian	Modified SERVQUAL (5)	28 statements 7-point Likert scale

Table 6.3 (continued): Study observations 'O'

Authors	Type of data collection	Service experienced (elapsed time between service and data collection)	Study location	SERVQUAL (dimensions)	Measure
Keirl and Mitchell [1990]	Personal interviews	-	United Kingdom	Modified SERVQUAL (10)	35 statements 7-point Likert scale
Lapierre [1993]	Personal interviews (managers) Mailed questionnaire (client)	Participation in project management within less than three years	Quebec Canada	Original SERVQUAL (10)	41 statements on perceptions 7-point Likert scale
Lévesque and McDougall [1992]	Written questionnaire completed on university site	Knowledgeable and experienced with financial institutions	Ontario Canada	SERVQUAL (5)	22 paired statements (expectations and perceptions) 7-point Likert scale
Mangold and Babakus [1991]	Mailed questionnaire No follow up	Patients discharged from hospital within the previous 12 months	South-West U.S.A.	Modified SERVQUAL (5)	41 paired statements (expectations and perceptions) 5-point Likert scale
Morgan [1990]	Mailed questionnaire No follow up	-	United Kingdom	Modified SERVQUAL (5)	9 statements 5-point Likert scale
Parasuraman *et al.* [1988]	Written questionnaire completed on site	Used the service in the past three months	Large metropolitan area in the Southwest of U.S.A. (first study) Major metropolitan area from the East U.S.A. (2nd study)	Original SERVQUAL (10) Reduced to (5)	97 paired statements (expectations and perceptions) 34 paired statements (expectations and perceptions) 22 paired statements (SERVQUAL) 7-point Likert scale
Parasuraman *et al.* [1991]	Mailed questionnaire to clients Electronic mail questionnaire to managers and employees Follow up by postal card two weeks after first mailing	-	U.S.A.	Modified SERVQUAL (5)	22 statements on expectations by clients completed by managers Measure of clients expectations scores and perceptions Perception evaluation of managers and employees 7-point Likert scale

Table 6.3 (continued): Study observations 'O'

Authors	Type of data collection	Service experienced (Elapsed time between service and data collection)	Study location	SERVQUAL (dimensions)	Measure
Peyrot *et al.* [1993]	Written question-naire given after ex-amination to be completed at home and returned by mail (stamp return enve-lope addressed to an independent evalua-tion organization) Coffee mug given as an inducement to participate in the study	After examination	Small city in Mid Atlantic Region U.S.A.	Modified SERVQUAL (5)	19 statements 4-point Likert Semantic differen-tial and nominal scale
Reidenbach and Sandifer-Smallwood [1990]	Phone survey Two calls for non-respondents	Service user within the past 12 months	South-East U.S.A.	Modified SERVQUAL (10)	41 paired statements (expectations and perceptions) 5-point Likert scale Bi-polar 5-points to evaluate percep-tion, satisfaction and willingness to recommend the service
Saleh and Ryan [1991]	Personal interviews in the presence of two researchers Written question-naire and interviews with staff manage-ment	Guests staying at the hotel in the summer of 1989	West-Canadian	Modified SERVQUAL (5)	33 paired statements (expectations and perceptions) 5-point Likert scale

The Type of Study 'T'

The most important source of contextual variation comes from factors related to the purpose of the investigation. A study's objectives determine to a great extent the units and the observations of the study. In fact, U, O and T should be consis-tent. The objectives of a study are created by the researcher working within a given theoretical and practical background. With regard to SERVQUAL investigations, three general categories of objectives can be identified: (1) methodological investi-gations mainly focusing on reliability and validity, (2) studies interested in in-creasing the knowledge of the concept of service quality measurement, and (3) managerial applications of SERVQUAL.

Parasuraman *et al.* [1988] were concerned with the external validity of SERVQUAL as were others who wished to replicate their findings under different contexts [Babakus and Mangold, 1992; Carman, 1990; Cronin and Taylor, 1992; Fick and Ritchie, 1991; Finn and Lamb, 1991; Lévesque and McDougall, 1992]. However, when one refers back to the U and O contextual factors explored above, each of these surveys developed a fairly unique protocol, and in many cases U and O were inconsistent with T. For instance, Carman [1990], clearly states that the main interest was to assess to what extent SERVQUAL dimensions are generic and to what extent they are adaptable to different types of services. According to this purpose, the type of respondents and services employed differed from those of Parasuraman *et al.* [1988]. However, the sampling procedure, the number of SERVQUAL dimensions measured and the elapsed time between service and measurement should theoretically have been the same as those of Parasuraman *et al.* [1988]. This was not the case. In addition, Carman [1990] only measured customer expectations for the student placement centre. The overall methodological differences between these two studies suggests that any comparison with regard to their purpose is risky. To what extent can one conclude about the external validity of SERVQUAL given these contextual variations?

SERVQUAL studies, whose objective is to advance knowledge concerning service quality assessment, have dealt with two issues. Firstly, to what extent does SERVQUAL actually measure the construct of service quality? For instance, Cronin and Taylor [1992] challenge the validity of the disconfirmation paradigm on which SERVQUAL is built. They suggest that service quality, insofar as it relates to the prediction of future behaviour, need only be assessed by measuring the customer's perceptions of service performance, and that questions on expectations are redundant. Their conclusion is based on data indicating that the perceptions of service performance (SERVPERF) predict the customer's global judgement of overall service quality just as well as measuring both expectations and perceptions (SERVQUAL). According to Cronin and Taylor [1992; 1994], the global judgement of service quality is more an attitude that influences satisfaction and it is the level of satisfaction that subsequently affects the customer's purchase intentions.

The second issue relates to a criticism which states that SERVQUAL measures only the functional and not the technical aspect of service quality [Babakus and Mangold, 1992; Finn and Lamb, 1991; Freeman and Dart, 1993]. However, this criticism may not be justified for the following reasons. In the validation studies, SERVQUAL was shown to be positively correlated to an attitude of satisfaction, to a willingness to recommend the service and to future purchasing intentions. Recalling that technical quality refers to 'what' is the basic nature of the service given rather than 'how' it is delivered [Grönroos, 1984], it is difficult to conceive that these positive correlations exist without the customer considering the technical aspect of service quality in their SERVQUAL responses.

Finally, it is surprising how little attention has been devoted to the objective of evaluating the applied managerial usefulness of SERVQUAL. The vast majority of the studies reviewed in this paper treat the managerial aspects of SERVQUAL on a purely theoretical basis. In terms of useful managerial information, one can only mention that Mangold and Babakus [1991] and Saleh and Ryan [1991] attempted to demonstrate differences among administrators, service deliverers and clients using SERVQUAL. Also, Parasuraman *et al.* [1991], referring to the Gap approach, found only weak correlations between the four organizational gaps and the SERVQUAL evaluation of the customer's global judgement of service quality.

Conclusion

SERVQUAL was developed as an instrument to improve the management of service quality [Parasuraman *et al.*, 1986, 1988]. If one agrees with the statement that "If you can't measure it you can't manage it" [Garvin, 1993] then one must conclude that the objective of SERVQUAL has not been achieved. Any such measuring instrument must first satisfy basic methodological criteria. SERVQUAL has been shown to be reasonably reliable and the construct validity was based on a sound conceptual foundation (i.e., the disconfirmation paradigm). However, the validity of the disconfirmation paradigm itself has been challenged in empirical investigations [Boulding *et al.*, 1993; Cronin and Taylor, 1993, 1994; Teas, 1993, 1994].

Based on the epistemological notion of 'contextuality', we question both the relevance of a universal scale to measure quality and the drawing of direct comparisons between empirical investigations without taking contextuality into account. The present analysis reveals that studies of SERVQUAL tend to be unique in terms of the units of study (U), the study observations (O) and the type of study (T). For instance, when we look at both the statistical and non-statistical measurement errors related to U, O and T, it becomes obvious that these error terms are always unique to a specific investigation.

Our contention is that research studies on service quality should demonstrate consistency among U, O and T. In addition, they should focus on the nomological dimensions of the construct. By defining what it is and what it is not, and by differentiating this construct from closely related concepts such as value, satisfaction, and customer behaviour, the marketing community will be able to develop a more firmly grounded model for constructing frameworks for measuring service quality.

References

Babakus, E. and W.G. Mangold, 1992, 'Adapting the SERVQUAL Scale to Hospital Services: An Empirical Investigation', *Health Service Research*, 26 (6), pp.768-786.

Bell, C.R. and R. Zemke, 1991, 'Commitment to Service Is Good Strategy', *Hospitals*, 65 (9), pp.56.

Berry, L.L. and A. Parasuraman, 1991, *Marketing Services, Competing Through Quality*, New York: The Free Press/Division of MacMillan Inc.

Berry, L.L., D.R. Bennett and C.W. Brown, 1989, *Service Quality: A Profit Strategy for Financial Institutions*, Dow Jones-Irwin.

Boulding, W., A. Kalra, R. Staelin and V.A. Zeithaml, 1993, 'A Dynamic Process Model of Service Quality: From Expectations to Behavioral Intentions', *Journal of Marketing Research*, 30, pp.7-27.

Bojanic, D.C., 1991, 'Quality Measurement in Professional Services Firms', *Journal of Professional Services Marketing*, 7 (2), pp.27-36.

Brown, T.J., G.A. Churchill, Jr. and J.P. Peter, 1993, 'Improving the Measurement of Service Quality', *Journal of Retailing*, 69 (1), pp.127-147.

Cannel, C., D. Oksenberg and J. Converse, 1977, 'Striving for Response Accuracy: Experiments in New Interviewing Technique', *Journal of Marketing Research*, 14, pp.306-315.

Carman, J.M., 1990, 'Consumer Perceptions of Service Quality: An Assessment of the SERVQUAL Dimensions', *Journal of Retailing*, 66 (1), pp.33-55.

CronbachH, L.J., 1986, 'Social Inquiry by and for Earthlings', in D.W. Fiske and R.A. Shweder (eds.), *Metatheory in Social Science Pluralisms and Subjectivities*, Chicago and London: The University of Chicago Press.

Cronin, J.J. and S.A. Taylor, 1992, 'Measuring Service Quality: A Reexamination and Extension', *Journal of Marketing*, 56, pp.55-68.

Cronin, J.J. and S.A. Taylor, 1994, 'SERVPERF Versus SERVQUAL: Reconciling Performance-Based and Perceptions-Minus-Expectations Measurement of Service Quality', *Journal of Marketing*, 58, pp.125-131.

Crosby, P.B., 1979, *Quality is Free*, New York: New American Library.

Crosby, P.B., 1984, *Quality without Tears*, New York: New American Library.

Crosby, P.B., 1989, *Let's Talk Quality, 96 Questions You Always Wanted to ask Phil Crosby*, McGraw-Hill Publishing Company.

Csipak, J., 1991, 'The Impact of Channel Structure and Consumers's Involvement on Perceived Service Quality: An Empirical Investigation', Doctoral Thesis, Université du Québec à Montréal, December.

Deming, W.E., 1960, *Sample Designs in Business Research*, New York: John Wiley and Sons.

Deming, W.E., 1988, *Qualité: La Révolution du Management*, Translated by Jean-Marie Gogue, Paris: Economica.

Feigenbaum, A.V., 1961, *Total Quality Control — Engineering and Management — The Technical and Managerial Field for Improving Product Quality Including its Reliability and Reducing Operating Costs & Losses*, McGraw-Hill Book Company Inc.

Feigenbaum, A.V., 1985, *Total Quality Control*, 3rd.ed., New York: McGraw-Hill.

Fick, G.R. and J.R.B. Ritchie, 1991, 'Measuring Service Quality in the Travel and Tourism Industry', *Journal of Travel Research*, Fall, pp.2-9.

Finn, D.W. and C.W. Lamb, 1991, 'An Evaluation of the SERVQUAL Scales in a Retailing Setting', *Advances in Consumer Research*, 18), pp.483-490.

Freeman, K.D. and J. Dart, 1993, 'Measuring the Perceived Quality of Professional Business Services', *Journal of Professional Services Marketing*, 9 (1), pp.27-47.

Garvin, D.A., 1988, *Managing Quality*, New York: The Free Press.

Garvin, D.A., 1993, 'Building a Learning Organization', *Harvard Business Review*, pp.78-91.

Grönroos, C., 1984, 'A Service Quality Model and Its Marketing Implications', *European Journal of Marketing*, 18 (4), pp.36-44.

Grönroos, C., 1988, 'Service Quality: The Six Criteria of Good Perceived Service Quality', *Review of Business*, 9 (3), pp.10-13.

Grönroos, C., 1990a, *Service Management and Marketing, Managing the Moment of Truth in Service Competition*, Massachusetts: Lexington Books.

Grönroos, C., 1990b, 'Marketing redefined', *Management Decision*, 28 (8), pp.5-9.

Gummesson, E. and C. Grönroos, 1987, 'Quality of Services - Lessons From The Products Sector', in C.Surprenant (ed.), *Add Value To Your Service* /American Marketing Association, pp.35-39.

Haywood-Farmer, J. and J. Nollet, 1991, *Service Plus Effective Service Management*, Édition Morin.

Ishikawa, K., 1985, *What is Total Quality Control? The Japanese Way*, translated by David J.Lu, New Jersey: Prentice-Hall/Englewood Cliffs.

Ishikawa, K., 1990, *Introduction to Quality control*, Japon: 3A Corporation.

Juran, J.M., 1982, *Upper Management and Quality*, New York: Juran Institute.

Juran, J.M., 1987a, *La Qualité dans les Services*, in codiffusion Eyrolles (eds), Translated by Monique Sperry, Paris: Afnor/Juran Institute.

Juran, J.M., 1987b, 'Quality Circles in the West', *Quality Progress*, September, pp.60-61.

Juran, J.M., 1992, *Quality by Design, the New Steps for Planning Quality into Goods and Service*, New York: The Free Press/Division of MacMillan Inc.

Juran, J.M. and F.M. Gryna, Jr., 1980, *Quality Planning and Analysis*, New York: McGraw-Hill Book Company.

Keirl, C. and P. Mitchell, 1990, 'How to Measure Industrial Service Quality', *Industrial Marketing Digest*, January-March, pp.35-46.

Knisely, G., 1979, 'Comparing Marketing Management in Package Goods and Service Organizations', in J.E.G.Bateson (2nd ed.), *Managing Services Marketing: Text and Readings*, 1992, Part I, Chapter 1, Introduction, Article 1.2, pp.26-47.

Lapierre, J., 1993, 'The Quality-Value Relationship in the Process for Evaluating Professional Services: the Case of Consulting Engineering', Doctoral Thesis, Université du Québec à Montréal, September.

Lévesque, T. and G.H.G. McDougall, 1992, 'Measuring Service Quality: An Assessment of the SERVQUAL Scale', In C.Duhaime (ed.), *Conférence de l'Association des Sciences Administratives du Canada*, Marketing, pp.127-136.

Mangold, W.G. and E. Babakus, 1991, 'Service Quality: The Front-Stage vs. the Back-Stage Perspective', *The Journal of Services Marketing*, 5 (4), pp.59-70.

Morgan, N.A., 1990, 'Corporate legal Advice and Client Quality Perceptions', *Marketing Intelligence and Planning*, 8 (6), pp.33-40.

Normann, R., 1991, *Service Management: Strategy and Leadership in Service Businesses*, (2nd ed.), New York: John Wiley and Sons.

Oliver, R.L., 1977, 'Effect of Expectation and Disconfirmation on Post-Exposure Product Evaluation: An Alternative Interpretation', *Journal of Applied Psychology*, 62), pp.480-486.

Oliver, R.L., 1980, 'A Cognitive Model of the Antecedents and Consequences of Satisfaction Decisions', *Journal of Marketing*, 17, pp.460-469.

Parasuraman, A., L.L. Berry and V.A. Zeithaml, 1991, 'Understand Customer Expectations of Service', *Sloan Management Review*, 32 (3), pp.39-48.

Parasuraman, A., V.A. Zeithaml and L.L. Berry, 1985, 'A Conceptual Model of Service Quality and Its Implications for Future Research', *Journal of Marketing*, 49, pp.41-50.

Parasuraman, A., V. Zeithaml and L.L. Berry, 1986, 'SERVQUAL: A Multiple-Item Scale for Measuring Customer Perceptions of Service Quality', *Marketing Science Institute*, Working Paper, August.

Parasuraman, A., V.A. Zeithaml and L.L. Berry, 1988, 'SERVQUAL: A Multi-Item Scale for Measuring Consumer Perceptions Service Quality', *Journal of Retailing*, 64 (1), pp.12-40.

Parasuraman, A., V.A. Zeithaml and L.L. Berry, 1994, 'Reassessment of Expectations as a Comparison Standard in Measuring Service Quality: Implications for Further Research', *Journal of Marketing*, 58, pp.111-124.

Perrien, J., P. Filiatrault and L. Ricard, 1993, 'The Implementation of Relationship Marketing in Commercial Banking', *Industrial Marketing Management*, 22), pp.141-148.

Peyrot, M., P.D. Cooper and D. Schnapf, 1993, 'Consumer Satisfaction and Perceived Quality of Outpatient Health Services', *Journal of Health Care Marketing*, Winter), pp.24-33.

Reidenbach, R.E. and B. Sandifer-Smallwood, 1990, 'Exploring Perceptions of Hospital Operations by a Modified SERVQUAL Approach', *Journal of Health Care Marketing*, 10 (4), pp.47-55.

Saleh, F., and C. Ryan, 1991, 'Analysing Service Quality in the Hospitality Industry Using the SERVQUAL Model', *The Services Industries Journal*, 11 (3), pp.324-343.

Teas, R.K., 1993, 'Expectations, Performance Evaluation, and Consumers' Perceptions of Quality', *Journal of Marketing*, 57, pp.18-34.

Teas, R.K., 1994, 'Expectations as a Comparison Standard in Measuring Service Quality: An Assessment of a Reassessment', *Journal of Marketing*, 58, pp.132-139.

Zeithaml, V.A., A. Parasuraman and L.L. Berry, 1990, *Delivering Quality Service, Balancing Customer Perceptions and Expectations*, New York: The Free Press.

Zeithaml, V.A., L.L. Berry and A. Parasuraman, 1993, 'The Nature and Determinants of Customer Expectations of Service', *Journal of the Academy of Marketing Science*, 21, pp.1-12.

7

The Foundations of Research on the Quality of Professional Services to Organisations

Jozée Lapierre[1] and Pierre Filiatrault[2]

This article examines the foundations of research on service quality. An extensive review of the literature on service quality reveals that the development of knowledge and research on service quality has been marked by three waves of research. A comparison is made of the dimensions used by the Nordic [Grönroos, 1984, 1988] and the American [Parasuraman, Zeithaml and Berry, 1985, 1986, 1988, 1994; Parasuraman, Berry and Zeithaml, 1991, 1993] schools of thought to evaluate service quality. The comparative analysis allows us to bridge the gap between the two schools of thought. Following an in-depth analysis of service quality variables and their operationalisation, the authors point out that specifically two determinants of quality, competence and reliability, must be considered and adapted to evaluate the quality of professional services.

Introduction

The marketing of services as an academic field of its own has been, without any doubt, legitimised [Fisk, Brown and Bitner, 1993; Berry and Parasuraman, 1993]. While Fisk *et al.* [1993] have tracked the evolution of the 'general' services marketing literature in describing three stages [pre-1980, 1980-85, and 1986-93], Berry and Parasuraman [1993] have used the case study method to describe the development of the academic sub-discipline of services marketing in the United States between 1970 and 1990. In the last decade, much attention was given by researchers to the topic of service quality [e.g., Grönroos, 1984; Parasuraman *et al.*, 1985]. Service quality has attracted the interest not only of academics, but also of practitioners as it potentially offered solutions to pragmatic and managerial problems as ev-

1   Assistant Professor, Department of Mathematics and Industrial Engineering, École Polytechnique de Montréal, 2900 Boulevard Édouard-Montperit, C.P. 6079, Succursale Centre-ville, Montréal, Québec, Canada, H3C 2A7.
2   Professor, School of Business Administration, Université du Québec à Montréal, C.P. 8888, Succursale Centre-ville, Montréal, Québec, Canada, H3C 4R2.

idenced earlier by Schmalensee, Bernhardt and Gust [1985], who stated that: "Service quality is a factor that distinguishes those firms that are highly successful from those that are merely average". Later on, the need to better understand service quality was also recognised as being essential for professional service firms: "As competition and customer sensitivity intensify, professional service providers are becoming increasingly concerned with quality of their offering" [Hall and Elliott, 1993]. The theoretical and empirical literature dealing with professional services is far less developed than that of more traditional services. In fact, only few efforts have been made to investigate business-to-business professional services quality [e.g., Freeman and Dart, 1993; Lapierre, 1993].

This chapter examines the foundations of research on service quality focusing on the evaluation of quality. It compares the dimensions used to evaluate service quality according to two schools of thought and draws implications for the evaluation of the quality of professional services to businesses. The general objective of this article is thus to investigate the professional service quality evaluation process by comparing the research frameworks associated with the two main schools of thought on service quality, in the context of professional services rendered to businesses.

Research on Service Quality

Following an extensive review of the literature, we identified the research carried out into the evaluation of service quality in general, and professional services quality specifically. Professional services are a subset which is differentiated from other services by being mainly advisory and being operated by skilled professionals [Gummesson, 1979]. Table 7.1 presents a list of authors classified in accordance with the two main parameters taken into account in the evaluation of quality, i.e., process & results dimensions and service dimensions.

The first column outlines service quality studies that focused mainly on the final process and results dimensions. Even though two generic service quality dimensions (technical quality and functional quality) were put forward explicitly by Grönroos [1984], some earlier authors used them implicitly to highlight aspects of service quality associated with the final process and results. The second column presents service quality studies that are related to the service dimensions put forward mainly by Parasuraman *et al.* [1985, 1986, 1988, 1991, 1993, 1994]. A similar phenomenon is found with regard to the service quality dimensions approach. Again, some earlier researchers used service dimensions in their research on service quality. Table 7.1 also indicates whether the study reported is rather empirical or theoretical, and whether the substantive domain refers to services in general or professional services, whose users are either consumers or organisations.

A brief look at Table 7.1 reveals that most of the research focusing on the process and results of the delivery of services, and using implicitly or explicitly the generic technical and functional service quality dimensions [Grönroos, 1984] tends to be more theoretical. It is also more concerned with general or traditional services, which are rendered mostly to individual customers. On the other hand, research that focuses more specifically on service quality dimensions [Parasuraman *et al.*, 1985, 1986, 1988, 1991, 1993, 1994] is mainly empirical and the services under investigation are both general and professional services. Most of the latter empirical research, however, deals with consumers rather than organisations.

Table 7.1 Summary of research on services and professional services quality

Process and Results Dimensions		Service Dimensions	
Lovelock and Young [1979]	TSC	Sarkar and Saleh [1974]	EPC
Czepiel [1980]	TSC	Albert and Pearson [1983]	EPC
Booms and Nyquist [1981]	TS/PC	Hull and Burns [1984]	EPO
Gummesson [1981b]	TPO		
Quelch and Asch [1981]	EPC		
Zeithaml [1981]	TS/PC	*Parasuraman et al. [1985, 1986,*	
Lewis and Booms [1983]	TSC	*1988, 1991, 1993, 1994]*	*ESC*
Grönroos [1984]	*ES/PC*	Cravens *et al.* [1985]	EPO
		Jackson *et al.* [1985]	EPC
		Knoll and Hoffman [1986]	TSC
Becker [1985]	TPC	Andrews *et al.* [1987]	TSC
Watson [1986]	TPO	Baumgarten and Hensel [1987]	EPC
Crosby and Stephens [1987]	ESC	Lindqvist [1987]	ESC
Grönroos [1987]	TSC	Little and Myers [1987]	EPC
Judd [1987]	TSO	Day *et al.* [1988]	EPC/O
Kelley [1987]	TSC	Teas [1988]	ESO
King [1987]	TSC	Hedvall and Paltschik [1989]	EPC
Wheatley [1987]	TPO	Carman [1988, 1990]	ES/PC
Lindqvist [1987]	ESC	Bojanic [1991]	EPC
Edvardsson [1988]	EPO	Bolton and Drew [1991,a,b]	ESC
Teas [1988]	ESO	Consulting Engineers Ass. [1991]	TPC/O
Lehtinen and Lehtinen [1991]	ESC	Nha [1991]	ESC
Lapierre [1993]	EPO	Babakus and Boller [1992]	ESC
		Cronin and Taylor [1992, 1994]	ESC
		Boulding *et al.* [1993]	ESC
		Freeman and Dart [1993]	EPO
		Lapierre [1993]	EPO
		Teas [1993, a, b, 1994]	ESC
		Brown *et al.* [1993]	ESC

Legend:	E = Empirical study
	T = Theoretical study
	S = Services in general
	P = Professional services
	C = Consumers
	O = Organisations

The first wave of research on service quality is closely linked with the conceptual works of Grönroos [1984] and Parasuraman *et al.* [1985], who kindled the concern for service quality. The major purpose of the seminal work of these pioneer researchers was first and foremost to clarify the definition of the quality construct in services marketing and to conceptualise it [Grönroos, 1984; Parasuraman *et al.* 1985, 1986, 1988]. The latter went a step further than Grönroos by developing a measuring instrument, the well-known SERVQUAL. These two research streams have subsequently given rise to a considerable body of literature, as evidenced by Table 7.1.

The second wave of research has drawn mostly on Grönroos' work and tested the importance of two generic dimensions, i.e., the technical and functional aspects of quality [e.g., Crosby and Stephens, 1987; Kelley, 1987]. Some authors [e.g., Lapierre, 1993; Hedvall and Paltschik, 1989; Lindqvist, 1987] have even used both the technical and functional quality [Grönroos, 1984] and the service quality dimensions [Parasuraman *et al.*, 1985]. The specific purpose of this second wave of research, which has drawn mainly on the work of Parasuraman *et al.* [1985, 1986, 1988], was replication in different general and professional services contexts. The nature of these studies was specifically at the level of the substantive domain [Brinberg and McGrath, 1985].

More recently, some authors have scrutinised and criticised a number of issues related to service quality evaluation, examining conceptual and methodological problems. The purpose of this third wave of research is, among other things, to test the real value of operationalising service quality in terms of expectations and perceptions, i.e., evaluating the gap model of Parasuraman *et al.* [1985, 1986, 1988, 1991, 1993, 1994] in comparison with other frameworks [e.g., Teas, 1993a, b, 1994; Brown *et al.*, 1993; Cronin and Taylor, 1992, 1994; Boulding, Kalra, Staelin and Zeithaml, 1993]. Some authors also questioned the stability of the dimensions of SERVQUAL as well as the mix of positive and negative statements [e.g., Cronin and Taylor, 1992, 1994; Lapierre, 1993; Babakus and Boller, 1992; Carman, 1988, 1990]. Other researchers are probing the integration of service quality research with attitude, value, satisfaction, behavioural intentions and monetary price research [e.g., Boulding *et al.*, 1993; Lapierre, 1993; Cronin and Taylor, 1992; Bolton and Drew, 1991a, b; Gorn, Tse and Weinberg, 1990].

The first and most important result of all this research on service quality has been the recognition of two complementary schools of thought, which have stimulated two streams of research and resulted in a rapid build-up of the body of knowledge. In the language of Brinberg and McGrath [1985], Grönroos' [1984] contribution has been mostly in the conceptual domain, whereas Parasuraman *et al.* [1985, 1986, 1988, 1991, 1993, 1994] have provided insights into both the conceptual and methodological domains.

The results of the works of the second wave of research draw specifically on the technical and functional quality approach and show that given the nature of services (intangibility, simultaneity of production and consumption, and heterogeneity), functional quality is very important, often more important than technical quality [Grönroos, 1984]. Functional quality is critically important because it allows differentiation, whereas technical quality often does not. On the other hand, the second wave of research that replicated SERVQUAL has shown the unstable character of the dimensions, whether it be the five or ten dimensions model. In fact, the structure of the dimensions of the model of Parasuraman *et al.* [1986, 1988] are seldom identical [e.g., Carman, 1988, 1990; Hedvall and Paltschik, 1989; Day, Denton and Hickner, 1988; Cravens, Dielman and Harrington, 1985].

Finally, the third wave research is of another nature. These studies have given rise to a more complex stream of research which has even more carefully scrutinised and criticised the conceptual and methodological domains of service quality research. Even Parasuraman *et al.* [1991] have been critical with regard to their own measuring instrument. Other researchers [e.g., Brown *et al.*, 1993; Teas, 1993a, b; Cronin and Taylor, 1992; Babakus and Boller, 1992; Carman, 1988, 1990] have carefully examined SERVQUAL and believe that there exist major flaws in the conceptualisation and operationalisation of service quality. Consequently, Brown *et al.* [1993], Teas [1993a, b], and Cronin and Taylor [1992] have developed and empirically tested alternatively perceived quality models that address the problems of the traditional framework. *criticism of SERVQUAL.*

Bridging the Gap Between the Two Schools of Thought

The extensive reviews of the literature by Lapierre [1993][3] and by Fisk *et al.* [1993] reveal that the two theoretical frameworks that are the best known and most used in the service quality research originates from two main schools of thought. The Nordic school of thought of service quality is mainly represented by Grönroos [1984, 1987, 1988, 1990, 1992a, b, 1993], whereas Parasuraman *et al.* [1985, 1986, 1988, 1991, 1993, 1994] have assumed leadership of the American school of thought.

Although Grönroos had already proposed the two generic dimensions (technical quality and functional quality) in 1984, it was not until 1988 that he specifically formulated a set of determining factors that can be compared with those of Parasuraman *et al.* [1988]. Grönroos [1988] suggested the following six criteria: professionalism and skills; attitudes and behaviour; accessibility and flexibility; reliability and trustworthiness; reputation and credibility; and recovery. These criteria, with the exception of recovery, may be linked to those of Parasuraman *et al.* [1988]. To the best of our knowledge, no empirical research has yet explicitly measured service quality using only Grönroos' [1988] criteria. *6 Ds link to PZBs'*

In their first study, Parasuraman *et al.* [1985] proposed that customers use ten criteria to evaluate service quality: tangibility, responsiveness, assurance, empathy, credibility, accessibility, courtesy, understanding/knowledge of the customers, communication and competence. The following year, they proposed a more parsimonious model with only five criteria: tangibility, reliability, responsiveness, assurance and empathy [Parasuraman *et al.* 1986]. The majority of empirical studies conducted on professional services quality have been influenced by the approach of Parasuraman *et al.*, and have used the SERVQUAL scale accordingly [e.g., Freeman and Dart, 1993; Bojanic, 1991; Carman, 1990, 1988; Hedvall and Paltschik, 1989; Day *et al.*, 1988; Little and Myers, 1987; Cravens *et al.*, 1985; Jackson, Brown and Keith, 1985]. *10 Ds → 5 Ds*

The recent service quality literature has identified major shortcomings in respect of the conceptualisation of service quality as suggested by Parasuraman *et al.* [1985, 1986, 1988, 1991, 1993, 1994;].

We will now look into the nature of service quality dimensions by comparing the components proposed by these two service quality schools of thought. This will be

---

3   The review of the literature was updated before the writing of this article.

two schools

followed by a discussion of the implications of these underlying dimensions for research on the quality of professional services to organisations.

A Comparative Analysis

The following comparative analysis uses Grönroos [1984] generic service quality dimensions (technical and functional quality) as a pivot to bridge the gap between the Nordic and the American schools of thought on service quality (Table 7.2).

3DS

There are basically two generic dimensions. The functional dimension is the result of interactions between service providers and their customers, whereas the technical dimension is based upon non-interactive elements [Grönroos and Gummesson, 1986].

The ten dimensions of the model of Parasuraman *et al.* [1985] have been broken down according to the generic dimensions after careful analysis of the variables defined by the authors. We repeated the same analysis using PZB's five dimensions model [1986, 1988, 1991, 1993, 1994], followed by the criteria suggested by Grönroos [1988]. The image (below the dotted line) and the corresponding dimensions of the other models are considered to be part of functional quality for the purpose of this discussion.

Table 7.2 Comparison of service quality dimensions

Grönroos [1984]	Parasuraman *et al.* [1985]	Parasuraman *et al.* [1986, 1988, 1991, 1993, 1994]	Grönroos [1988]
Technical quality (What)	Competence Reliability (technical)	Assurance Reliability (technical)	Professionalism and skills
Functional quality (How)	Reliability (functional)	Reliability (functional)	Reliability and trustworthiness
	Responsiveness Courtesy	Responsiveness Assurance	{ Attitudes and behaviour {
	Security Tangibility	Assurance Tangibility	({ Accessibility and flexibility {
	Accessibility Communication Understanding	(Empathy { (	(
			Recovery
Image	Credibility	Assurance	Reputation and credibility

In-depth analysis of the variables and their operationalisation in the context of this comparative analysis reveals that two determinants of quality, competence and reliability are particularly problematical in the case of the quality of professional services. We will now address these two issues.

The Competence Determinant of Professional Services Quality
The first issue is concerned with competence as a determinant of the quality of professional services. Researchers interested in industrial marketing and professional services marketing have already shown that the interactive and non-interactive functions must be considered separately in organisational professional services [Håkansson, 1989; Grönroos and Gummesson, 1986; Gummesson, 1984]. This argument is also supported by the results of a focus group and ten in-depth interviews conducted with Quebec consulting engineers, which revealed that consulting engineers first and foremost used a technical language when talking about service quality [Lapierre, 1993].

According to Grönroos [1988], there is only one dimension in technical quality: professionalism and skills. When examining the model proposed by Parasuraman, Zeithaml and Berry in 1985, we find that the competence dimension corresponds to Grönroos' professionalism and skills dimension. However, in the models of Parasuraman *et al.* [1986, 1988, 1991, 1993, 1994], the competence dimension has become part of the assurance dimension, and, thus, relate to functional rather than technical quality. In our opinion, this does not reflect the reality of professional services, especially from the perspective of consulting engineers services.

In fact, acceptance of the five dimensions of Parasuraman *et al.* [1988, 1991, 1993, 1994] amounts to saying that the evaluation of quality relates only to the evaluation of the process, i.e., the functional quality. Thus, technical quality has *de facto* been set aside. Yet, we note that several empirical studies dealing with professional services rendered to both individual and organisational customers have recognised that competence is the most important factor for evaluating professional services quality [e.g., Day *et al.*, 1988; Baumgarten and Hensel, 1987; Little and Myers, 1987; Knoll and Hoffman, 1986; Cravens *et al.*, 1985; Albert and Pearson, 1983]. The results of these studies clearly suggest that the competence dimension should be distinguished from other dimensions subsumed under the assurance dimension, at least as far as organisational professional services are concerned.

Additionally, if we take a closer look at the meaning of competence in the latter research, we realise that it is definitely not concerned with functional quality (the How), but rather to technical quality (the What). Grönroos [1988] puts it this way: "The customers realize that the service provider, his employees, operational systems and physical resources, have the knowledge and skills required to solve their problems in a professional way". Furthermore, Parasuraman *et al.* themselves gave the following definition of competence in their 1985 article: "Possession of the required skills and knowledge to perform service". Finally, the industrial marketing literature [Saporta, 1989] also suggests that competence is directly associated with technical quality. In engineering parlance, competence means 'know-how'; in other words, the professional's knowledge and skills.

The Reliability Determinant of Professional Services Quality
A second issue related to the comparison of the works of Parasuraman *et al.*, [1985, 1986, 1988, 1991, 1993, 1994] and Grönroos [1984, 1988] pertains to reliability. On the one hand, this determinant constitutes one indivisible dimension in the models of Parasuraman *et al.* [1985, 1986, 1988, 1991, 1993, 1994]. They define it as "consistency of performance and dependability" [Parasuraman *et al.*, 1985] and "the ability to perform the promised service dependably and accurately" [Zeithaml, Parasuraman and Berry, 1990]. However, if we look at the statements included in the SERVQUAL measuring scale, we see that some statements clearly have a technical connotation, while others have a functional one. Indeed, analysis of the five statements relating to the customer's perceptions of service reliability, shows that statements 7 and 9 have a technical quality connotation, whereas statements 5, 6, and 8 have a functional quality connotation (Table 7.3).

Table 7.3 Reliability statements

Statement 5:	"When XYZ Co. promises to do something by a certain time, it does so" [Parasuraman *et al.*, 1988, 1991] has a **functional** quality connotation;
Statement 6:	"When you have a problem, XYZ Co. shows a sincere interest in solving it" [Parasuraman *et al.*, 1991] or "is sympathetic and reassuring" [Parasuraman *et al.* 1988] has a **functional** quality connotation;
Statement 7:	"XYZ Co. performs the service right the first time" [Parasuraman *et al.*, 1991] or "is dependable" [Parasuraman *et al.*, 1988] has a **technical** quality connotation;
Statement 8:	"XYZ Co. provides its service at the time it promises to do so" [Parasuraman *et al.*, 1988, 1991] has a **functional** quality connotation;
Statement 9:	"XYZ Co. insists on error-free records" [Parasuraman *et al.*, 1991] or "keeps its records accurately" [Parasuraman *et al.*, 1988] has a **technical** quality connotation.

The above reasoning is supported by empirical results of studies that have been carried out in the area of professional services, specifically those conducted in the fields of engineering and architecture [Gordon, Calantone and Di Benedetto, 1993; Lapierre, 1993; Association of Consulting Engineers of Quebec, 1990; Knoll and Hoffman, 1986; Cravens *et al.*, 1985; Sarkar and Saleh, 1974]. For example, these results highlight the importance of doing things right the first time, in an error-free manner (the technical quality dimension), corresponding to statements 7 and 9 of Parasuraman *et al.* [1991], as well as meeting deadlines (the functional quality dimension), corresponding to statements 5 and 8 in Parasuraman *et al.* [1991].

On the other hand, Grönroos [1988] combines reliability and trustworthiness into a unique dimension of functional quality which he defines as follows: "customers know that whatever takes place or has been agreed upon, they can rely on the service provider, its employees and systems, to keep promises and perform with the best interest of the customers at heart".

It follows from the foregoing that the dimensions of the Parasuraman *et al.* [1985, 1986, 1988, 1991, 1993, 1994] models must be modified for the purposes of a study that requires the technical quality and functional quality distinction, as in the case of many, if not most professional services. Accordingly, the important dimension of reliability should be divided into statements that relate to both technical and functional quality, in spite of the position of Grönroos [1988] and Edvardsson [1988], who argue that reliability is an element of functional quality.

Conclusion

The development of services marketing has aroused interest in this new academic field in general, and more specifically in research on service quality. This chapter is first concerned with the foundations of research on service quality focusing on the evaluation of quality.

Two schools of thought, the Nordic and the American schools, have influenced theoretical and empirical studies on service quality. The dimensions underlying service quality have been compared using as a pivot Grönroos' generic service quality dimensions to bridge the gap between the two schools. Two determinants of quality are problematical in the case of the quality of professional services: competence and reliability.

As regards competence, various researchers have argued that technical quality is an essential element of the quality of professional services, of which competence is an important determinant. By accepting the five dimensions of the PZB model, one puts aside technical quality in favour of functional quality, as competence becomes part of assurance. Like many other authors, we believe that this is incorrect in the case of the quality of professional services to organisations.

A second issue has to do with reliability which is a one-dimension determinant in the PZB model. In-depth analysis of the meaning of the variables operationalised in the SERVQUAL scale reveals that some statements have a technical while others have a functional quality connotation. We proposed that the reliability dimension be separated into technical and functional dimensions in the case of professional services.

Hence, the existing models of service quality must be adapted to the specificities of professional services. We recognise, however, the value of the conceptual work of Grönroos and Parasuraman, Zeithaml and Berry in the research and knowledge on service quality. It is hoped that the above discussion will contribute to the development of a universal model of service quality and, hence, to bridging the gap between the Nordic and the American schools of thought.

References

Albert, J.D. and T.D. Pearson, 1983, 'Marketing Professional Appraisal Services', *Appraisal Journal*, (April), pp.225-233.

Andrews, J.F., J.H. Drew English, M.J. and M. Rys, 1987, 'Service Quality Surveys in a Telecommunications Environment: An Integrating Force', in J.A. Czepiel, C.A. Congram and C.A. Shannaham, *The Service Challenge: Integrating for Competitive Advantage*, AMA, pp.27-31.

Association of Consulting Engineers of Quebec, 1990, *Analyse de la situation du génie-conseil québécois et axes d'orientations*, (June).

Babakus, E. and G.W. Boller, 1992, 'An Empirical Assessment of the SERVQUAL Scale', *Journal of Business Research*, 24, pp.253-268.

Baumgarten, S.S. and J.S. Hensel, 1987, 'Enhancing the Perceived Quality of Medical Service Delivery Systems', in C. Surprenant (ed.), *Add Value to Your Service*. AMA, pp.105-110.

Becker, B., 1985, 'The Six Most Frequently Asked Questions About Selling and Marketing Accounting Services', *Practical Accountant*, 18 (7) , pp.81-84.

Berry, L.L. and A. Parasuraman, 1993, 'Building a New Academic Field — The Case of Services Marketing', *Journal of Retailing*, 69 (1), pp.13-59.

Bojanic, D.C., 1991, 'Quality Measurement in Professional Services Firms', *Journal of Professional Services Marketing*, 17 (2), pp.27-36.

Bolton, R.N. and J.H. Drew, 1991a, 'A Multistage Model of Customers' Assessments of Service Quality and Value', *Journal of Consumer Research*, 17 (March), pp.375-84.

Bolton, R.N. and J.H. Drew, 1991b, 'A Longitudinal Analysis of the Impact of Service Changes on Customer Attitudes', *Journal of Marketing*, 55 (January), pp.1-9.

Booms, B.H. and J.L. Nyquist, 1981, 'Analyzing the Customer/Firm Communication Component of the Services Marketing Mix', in J. Donnelly and W. George (eds.), *Marketing of Services*, AMA, pp.172-177.

Boulding, W., A. Kalra, R. Staelin and V.A. Zeithaml, 1993, 'Dynamic Process of Service Quality: From Expectations to Behavioral Intentions', *Journal of Marketing Research*, 21 (February), pp.7-27.

Brinberg, D. and J.E. McGrath, 1985, *Validity and the Research Process*. Sage.

Brown, T.J., G.A. Churchill and J.P. Peter, 1993, 'Improving the Measurement of Service Quality', *Journal of Retailing*, 69 (1), pp.127-139.

Carman, J.M., 1990, 'Consumer Perceptions of Service Quality: An Assessment of the SERVQUAL Dimensions', *Journal of Retailing*, 66 (1), pp.33-55.

Carman, J.M., 1988, 'The Dimensions and Measurement of Service Quality: An Assessment of the SERVQUAL Dimensions', in L.L. Berry (ed.), *Marketing of Services*, Institut d'administration des entreprises, Université d'Aix-Marseille, France (IAE), pp.85-98.

Cravens, D.W., T.E. Dielman and C.G. Harrington, 1985, 'Using Buyers' Perceptions of Service Quality to Guide Strategy Development', in R.F. Lisch, G.T. Ford, G.L. Frazier, R.D. Howell, C.A. Ingene, M. Reillay and R.W. Stampfl, *AMA Educators' Proceedings*. (eds.), pp.297-301.

Cronin, J.J. and S.A. Taylor, 1994, 'SERVPERF Versus SERVQUAL: Reconciling Performance-Based and Perceptions-Minus-Expectations Measurement of Service Quality', *Journal of Marketing*, 58 (January), pp.125-131.

Cronin, J.J. and S.A. Taylor, 1992, 'Measuring Service Quality: A Reexamination and Extension', *Journal of Marketing*, 56 (July), pp.55-68.

Crosby, L.A. and N. Stephens, 1987, 'Effects of Relationship on Satisfaction, Retention, and Prices in the Life Insurance Industry', *Journal of Marketing Research*, XXIV (November), pp.404-411.

Czepiel, J.A., 1980, *Managing Customer Satisfaction in Consumer Service Businesses*. Cambridge, MA: Marketing Science Institute.

Day, E., L.L. Denton and J.A. Hickner, 1988, 'Clients' Selection and Retention Criteria: Some Marketing Implications for the Small CPA Firms', *Journal of Professional Services Marketing*, 3/4, pp.283-295.

Edvardsson, B., 1988, 'Service Quality in Customer Relationships: A Study of Critical Incidents in Mechanical Engineering Companies', *Services Industries Journal*, 8, No.4 (October), pp.427-445.

Fisk, R.P., S.W. Brown and M.J. Bitner, 1993, 'Tracking the Evolution of the Services Marketing Literature', *Journal of Retailing*, 69 (1), pp.61-103.

Freeman, K.D. and J. Dart, 1993, 'Measuring the Perceived Quality of Professional Business Services', *Journal of Professional Services Marketing*, 9 (1), pp.27-48.

Gordon, G.L., R.S. Calantone and C.A. DI Benedetto, 1993, 'Business-to-Business Service Marketing', *Journal of Business & Industrial Marketing*, 8 (1), pp.45-57.

Gorn, G.J., Tse, D.K. and C.B. Weinberg, 1990, 'The Impact of Free and Exaggerated Prices on Perceived Quality of Services', *Marketing Letters*, 2 (2), pp.99-110.

Grönroos, C., 1993, 'Towards a Third Phase in Service Quality Research. Challenges and Future Directions', in T.A. Swartz, D.E. Bowen and S.W. Brown (eds.), *Advances in Services Marketing and Management*. , 2, JAI (forthcoming).

Grönroos, C., 1992a, 'How Quality Came and Where It Is Going', in E. Scheuing and W. Christopher (eds.), *Handbook of Service Quality*, New York: AMACOM.

Grönroos, C., 1992b, 'Facing the Challenge of Service Competition: The Economics of Service', P. Kunst & J. Lemmink (eds.), in *Quality Management in Services*, Maastricht/Assen: Van Gorcum, pp.129-140.

Grönroos, C., 1990, *Service Management and Marketing*. Lexington Books.

Grönroos, C., 1988, 'Service Quality: The Six Criteria of Good Perceived Service Quality', *Review of Business*, St-John's University, 9 (3), pp.10-13.

Grönroos, C., 1987, 'Developing the Service Offering — A Source of Competitive Advantage', in C. Surprenant, *Add Value To Your Service*, AMA, pp.81-85

Grönroos, C., 1984, 'A Service Quality Model and its Marketing Implications', *European Journal of Marketing*, 18 (4), pp.36-44.

Grönroos, C. and E. Gummesson, 1986, 'Service Orientation in Industrial Marketing', in M. Venkatesan, D.M. Schmalensee and C. Marshall, *Creativity in Services Marketing: What's New, What Works, What's Developing*. AMA, pp.23-26.

Gummesson, E., 1984, *Beyond Services Marketing*. Research report presented at the Third Services Marketing Conference: AMA (September).

Gummesson, E., 1981b, 'The Marketing of Professional Services: 25 Propositions', in J. Donnelly and W. George (eds.), *Marketing of Services*. AMA, pp.108-112.

Håkansson, H., 1989, *International Marketing and Purchasing of Industrial Goods: An Interaction Approach*. John Wiley & Sons.

Hall, M.C. and K.M. Elliott, 1993, 'Expectations and Performance from Whose Perspective: A Note on Measuring Service Quality', *Journal of Professional Services Marketing*, 8 (2), pp.27-32.

Hedvall, M.B. and M. Paltschik, 1989, 'An Investigation In and Generation of Service Quality Concepts', in G.J. Avlonitis, N.K. Papavasiliou and A.G. Kouremenos (eds.), *Marketing Thought and Practice in the 1990s*. European Marketing Academy, 1, pp.373-483.

Hull, J. and R.G. Burns, 1984, 'Is NRC's QA Program Working?', *Quality Progress* (January), pp.29-33.

Jackson, D.W., S.W. Brown and J.E. Keith, 1985, 'Business Executives, Evaluations of Various Aspects of Outside Legal Services', in T.M. Bloch, G.D. Upah and V.A. Zeithaml (eds.), *Services Marketing in a Changing Environment*, AMA, pp.130-134.

Judd, V.C., 1987, 'Differentiate with the 5th P: People', *Industrial Marketing Management*, 16 (4), pp.241-247.

Kelley, S.W., 1987, *Managing Service Quality: The Organizational Socialization of the Service Employee and Customer*. UMI Dissertation Information Service, University of Kentucky.

King, C.A., 1987, 'A Framework for a Service Quality Assurance System,' *Quality Progress*, 20 (8), pp.27-32.

Knoll, L.N. and A.P. Hoffman, 1986, 'Strategic Market research — The Foundation for Growth: Case Study of a Professional Services Firm', in M. Venkatesan, D.M. Schmalensee and C. Marshall (eds.), *Creativity in Service Marketing*. AMA, pp.141-144.

Lapierre, J., 1993, *The Quality - Value Relationship in the Process for Evaluating Professional Services: The Case of Consulting Engineering*, Doctoral Dissertation, Université du Québec à Montréal.

Lehtinen, U. and J. Lehtinen, 1991, 'Two Approaches to Services Quality Dimensions', *The Service Industries Journal*, (3,) pp.287-303.

Lewis, R.C. and B.H. Booms, 1983, 'The Marketing Aspects of Service Quality', in L.L. Berry, G.L. Shostack and G.D. Upah (eds.), *Emerging Perspectives on Services Marketing*. AMA, pp.99-104.

Lindqvist, L.J., 1987, 'Quality and Service Value in the Consumption of Services', in C. Surprenant (ed.), *Add Value to Your Service: The Key to Success*, AMA, pp.17-20.

Little, M.W. and T.A. Myers, 1987, 'An Assessment of Home Buyer And Real Estate Broker Attitudes Toward Service Quality', *Journal of Professional Services Marketing*, 3 (1/2), pp.101-118.

Lovelock, C.H. and R. Young, 1979, 'Look to Consumers to Increase Productivity', *Harvard Business Review*, (May/June), pp.168-178.

Nha, N., 1991, 'Un modèle explicatif de l'évaluation de la qualité d'un service: une étude empirique', *Recherche et Applications en Marketing*, 6 (2), pp.83-97.

Parasuraman, A., L.L. Berry and V.A. Zeithaml, 1993, 'More on Improving Service Quality Measurement', *Journal of Retailing*, 69 (1), pp.140-147.

Parasuraman, A., L.L. Berry and V.A. Zeithaml, 1991, 'Refinement and Reassessment of the SERVQUAL Scale', *Journal of Retailing*, 67, No.4 (Winter), pp.420-450.

Parasuraman, A., V.A. Zeithaml and L.L. Berry, 1994, 'Reassessment of Expectations as a Comparison Standard in Measuring Service Quality: Implications for Further Research', *Journal of Marketing*, 58 (January), pp.111-124.

Parasuraman, A., V.A. Zeithaml and L.L. Berry, 1988, 'SERVQUAL: A Multiple-Item Scale for Measuring Customer Perceptions of Service Quality', *Journal of Retailing*, 64 (Spring), pp.12-40.

Parasuraman, A., V.A. Zeithaml and L.L. Berry, 1986, SERVQUAL: A Multiple-Item Scale for Measuring Customer Perceptions of Service Quality. Working Paper: Marketing Science Institute. Report No.86-108.

Parasuraman, A., V.A. Zeithaml and L.L. Berry, 1985, 'A Conceptual Model of Service Quality and Its Implications for Future Research', *Journal of Marketing*, 49 (Fall), pp.41-50.

Quelch, J.A. and S.B. Asch, 1981, 'Consumer Satisfaction with Professional Services', in J.H. Donnelly and W.R. George (eds.), *Marketing of Services*, AMA, pp.82-85.

Sarkar, A.K. and F.A. Saleh, 1974, 'The Buyer of Professional Services: An Examination of Some Key Variables in the Selection Process', *Journal of Purchasing & Materials Management*, 10 (1), pp.22-25.

Schmalensee, D.H., K. Bernhardt and N. Gust, 1985, 'Key to Successful Services Marketing: Customer Orientation, Creed, Consistency', in T.M. Bloch, G.D. Upah and V.A. Zeithaml (eds.), *Services Marketing in a Changing Environment*, AMA, pp.15-18.

Teas, R.K., 1994, 'Expectations as a Comparison Standard in Measuring Service Quality: An Assessment of a Reassessment', *Journal of Marketing*, 58 (January), pp.132-139.

Teas, R.K., 1993a, 'Consumer Expectations and the Measurement of Perceived Service Quality', *Journal of Professional Services Marketing*, 8 (2), pp.33-54.

Teas, R.K., 1993b, 'Expectations, Performance Evaluation, and Consumers' Perceptions of Quality', *Journal of Marketing*, 57 (October), pp.18-34.

Teas, R.K., 1988, 'An Analysis of the Determinants of Industrial Consumers' Perceptions of the Quality of Financial Services Marketing Relationships', *Journal of Professional Services Marketing*, (3/4), pp.71-88.

Watson, I., 1986, 'Managing the Relationships with Corporate Customers', *International Journal of Bank Marketing* (UK), 4 (1), pp.19-36.

Wheatley, E.W., 1987, 'Rainmakers, Mushrooms and Immaculate Conception: Internal Marketing for Professional Service Firm Associates', *Journal of Professional Services Marketing*, 2 (24), pp.73-82.

Zeithaml, V.A., 1981, 'How Consumer Evaluation Processes Differ Between Goods and Services', in J.H. Donnelly and W.R. George (eds.), *Marketing of Services*, AMA, pp.186-190.

Zeithaml, V.A., A. Parasuraman and L.L. Berry, 1990, *Delivering Quality Service*. New York: The Free Press.

8

On Service Quality Models, Service Quality Dimensions and Customers' Perceptions

Uolevi Lehtinen[1], Jukka Ojasalo[2] and Katri Ojasalo[3]

The objective of this study is to demonstrate if and how service quality dimensions used in well-known quality models show up when choosing different services. The examination of quality dimensions is based on five models of service quality.

This study focuses on commonly used and simple services in a dining restaurant, a pub, and a barber's shop. The research used a modified CIT method (Critical Incident Technique). The purpose in this study was to allow the interviewees to reveal their opinions about factors affecting service quality as freely as possible and without any leading. The interviewees were also allowed to describe any factor affecting service quality in any situation.

In the theoretical part of the study, we outlined a structural framework of dimensions which was used in the empirical part to categorise the data. In the empirical study, the three high-level dimensions (physical quality, interactive quality, and corporate quality) matched to all the case services, while the low-level dimensions of the models did not match well with any service. In the restaurant and pub, one-third of the low-level dimensions did not receive any empirical support. The results of this study indicate that multidimensional models cannot easily be generalised to a heterogeneous area such as service quality.

Objective

The objective of this study is, first, to demonstrate if and how service quality dimensions used in well-known quality models show up in different services. Empirically this means that we examine how dimensions appear in the expressions

---

1   Professor of Marketing at the University of Tampere, Finland.
2   Researcher at the Swedish School of Economics and Business Administration in Helsinki, Finland.
3   Researcher at the Swedish School of Economics and Business Administration in Helsinki, Finland.

used by interviewed customers to describe three general service sectors. In the theoretical part of the study we outline a structural framework of dimensions which is used in the empirical part to categorise the expressions of interviewees. The secondary objective is to outline possibilities and/or limitations for developing quality models.

Quality dimensions have been an essential basis of former theoretical and empirical studies concerning service quality. In this study the examination of quality dimensions is based on five well-known models of service quality: Armistead and Wampach [1988[, Grönroos [1990], Haywood-Farmer [1990], Lehtinen and Lehtinen [1982, 1991], and Zeithaml, Parasuraman and Berry [1985, 1990]. These models were chosen because they cover comprehensively existing service quality dimensions used in other models.

Dimensions of Quality

In this article we compare dimensions of different quality models and combine them into a common structural framework. In order to outline the basic structure of dimensions, we used the dimensions of Lehtinen and Lehtinen's quality model to classify those of other models. These dimensions were chosen to be the guiding framework of the study because of their extensive coverage as to other dimensions and (different) services. This may become more evident in the following analysis.

In Lehtinen and Lehtinen's three-dimensional model of service quality, the dimensions are related to the elements of the service production process (Lehtinen and Lehtinen, 1982 and 1991). The dimensions of this model are:

1. physical quality
2. interactive quality
3. corporate quality

Physical quality originates in the physical elements of service, such as physical product(s), and physical support needed in a service production process. Physical products can be defined as goods consumed during the service production process. Physical support is a framework that enables or facilitates the service production and consumption process. It consists of the environment and instruments. In this study, we also included accessibility, which in this context means a location and opening days/hours of a service company.

Interactive quality originates between the customer and interactive elements of a service organisation, i.e., contact personnel or physical equipment. In this study, interactive quality based on the four models is composed of eight dimensions: responsiveness, professionalism, behaviour, communication, understanding the customer, recovery, timeliness and speed, and reliability. *Responsiveness* is willingness to help customers and provide prompt service. *Behaviour* includes friendliness, politeness, respect, and consideration of contact personnel toward customers. *Communication* means keeping the customers informed in a language they can understand, and listening to them. *Understanding the customer* involves making personnel better aware of customer needs. In this context, *reliabil-*

ity means ability to perform the promised service dependably and accurately as well as in a confidential way. *Professionalism* as well as *timeliness and speed* are self-explanatory features of quality.

Corporate quality develops during the history of a service organisation, and refers to how customers and potential customers view the corporate entity and its units. It includes the corporation's image or profile (Lehtinen and Lehtinen, 1991). In this study, corporate quality is divided into two dimensions: corporate/local image and assurance. *Corporate/local image* is the reputation of the corporate entity and its units. It is also connected to the products of the corporation. *Assurance* involves both credibility and security. Credibility is composed of trustworthiness, believability, and honesty of a service organisation, and security means being free from danger or risk.

All of the above-mentioned models included tangibles and accessibility in the factors affecting customers' evaluation of service quality. Most dimensions affecting service quality in Table 8.1 belong to the interactive quality. These dimensions were included in at least three models. Corporate quality was the least represented dimension in various models; in addition to Lehtinen and Lehtinen's model, this issue was emphasised only by Grönroos (1991).

Some interpretations leading to the framework can be ambiguous. Thus, the classification of accessibility and assurance is not self-evident, and some interactive dimensions are correlated. However, we believe that this does not affect the totality of the framework.

Table 8.1 The framework of quality dimensions based on classification by Lehtinen and Lehtinen's three-dimensional model of service quality

	A-W	Gr	Ha	Z-P-B
PHYSICAL QUALITY				
1. Tangibles	X	X	X	X
2. Accessibility	X	X	X	X
INTERACTIVE QUALITY				
1. Responsiveness	X	X	-	X
2. Professionalism	-	X	X	X
3. Behaviour	-	X	X	X
4. Communication	X	-	X	X
5. Understanding the customer	X	-	X	X
6. Recovery	X	X	X	-
7. Timeliness and speed	X	-	X	-
8. Reliability	X	X	X	X
CORPORATE QUALITY				
1. Corporate/local image	-	X	-	-
2. Assurance	X	X	-	X

A-W = Armistead and Wampach
Gr = Grönroos
Ha = Haywood-Farmer
Z-P-B = Zeithaml, Parasuraman and Berry

Methodology

This exploratory study focuses on commonly used and simple services because we wanted to avoid a-typicality and complexity. Companies chosen for the study are a dining restaurant, a pub, and a barber's shop.

The purpose of the empirical study was to allow the interviewees to reveal their opinions about factors affecting service quality as freely as possible. The research uses a modified Critical Incident Technique (CIT). Whereas the original method is limited to service encounters that have really happened and that the interviewee has experienced, the CIT method in this study was modified: being not limited to their own experiences, the interviewees were allowed to tell about any factor affecting service quality in any other situation For example, they were allowed to tell about quality factors they consider ideal ("Describe your ideas about the ideal dining restaurant/pub/barber's shop"), or about service experiences they had heard of.

Fifteen customers (five of each case company) were interviewed. We were able to classify 146 quality expressions by the respondents, the term 'expression' covering a wide range of statements from one word comments to detailed descriptions.

We tried to interview a representative group of the case companies' customers with regard to age and sex. The interviewing and classifying techniques had been planned to increase reliability. The CIT-type questions provided a framework for the interviews. During all the interviews, a number of more detailed questions were asked when the interviewee did not give a clear and precise answer. Insinuating questions and remarks were avoided. All interviews were tape-recorded, and some written notes were made to describe feelings of the respondents. The interviews were transcribed before the analysis.

The interviewees were given ample time to think about and answer the questions, and were thus given the opportunity to reveal most of the main factors they thought affect service quality. Some repetition was used to test the consistency of the answers.

As to the reliability of the interpretation we followed the principle of the CIT method: the three researchers independently categorised the expressions of service quality mentioned by the respondents. Ninety-two per cent of the expressions were classified similarly (according to the CIT method 80% is sufficient). The remaining eight per cent of the expressions was classified jointly after some consideration.

Results of the Empirical Study

Service quality manifested itself in a large number of different expressions during the interviews. 146 expressions of the interviewees referring to quality dimensions are classified as shown in Table 8.2.

Table 8.2 The frequencies of expressions referring to quality dimensions in the framework

	Dining restaurant	Pub	Barber's shop	All
PHYSICAL QUALITY				
1. Tangibles	18	16	9	43
2. Accessibility	1	2	3	6
	19	18	12	49
INTERACTIVE QUALITY				
1. Responsiveness	3	2	0	5
2. Professionalism	0	1	7	8
3. Behaviour	10	5	9	24
4. Communication	0	0	5	5
5. Understanding the customer	3	2	8	13
6. Recovery	1	0	0	1
7. Timeliness and speed	4	4	2	10
8. Reliability	0	0	1	1
9. Other customers	4	9	1	14
	25	23	33	81
CORPORATE QUALITY				
1. Corporate/local image	4	6	4	14
2. Assurance	0	0	2	2
	4	6	6	16
Total	48	47	51	146

Quality expressions were divided into three main categories (physical quality, interactive quality, corporate quality). Partly because most dimensions of the models were linked to interaction, more than half of the expressions were related to interactive quality. As physical elements are concrete they are more understandable and, thus, easy to describe. Therefore, it is not surprising that one-third of all expressions was related to physical quality. Corporate quality also seemed to affect total service quality, although only 12% of all expressions related to this area. This is because corporate quality is not as easy to express as physical or interactive quality.

The framework seems to be best applicable to the barber's shop, where only two dimensions are without any listing (responsiveness and recovery). In the case of the dining restaurants and pub, this held true of four quality dimensions. However, there are only minor differences, especially when looking at the total scores per service.

Tangibles was clearly the dimension mentioned most often in the interviews. Interviewees easily remember and mention concrete service elements. Additionally, tangibles are composed of several parts, which obviously has an effect on the number of tangibles-related expressions. *Behaviour* was second as regards the number of expressions mentioned. Like tangibles, it is composed of a large number of different factors. Interestingly, *other customers* frequently appeared in expressions, although it was not an evident dimension in the models or our framework. Nevertheless, it was not unexpected. For example, Lehtinen and Lehtinen [1991] had already found that interaction between the customers of the service company is often a very important quality issue. *Image* was mentioned quite often in all service situations, which was in accordance with our expectations. *Understanding the customer* was fifth in number, closely followed by *timeliness* and *speed*. *Recovery* was not addressed in the interviews. Only one customer of a dining restaurant made mention of the importance of recovery for her evaluation of service quality. *Reliability* was mentioned only once, which is in contrast with other studies (Parasuraman, Zeithaml and Berry, 1988], in which reliability was by far the most important dimension.

Although we view many detailed results in Table 8.2 as being interesting, we expect that some of them would have different if our sample had been larger. Therefore, we emphasise the importance of the totality and main features of the results, which as a consequence of the number of expressions are expected to be fairly reliable.

Discussion

It is obvious that determining quality dimensions and operative determinants of quality derived from those dimensions is essential for a service organisation. After establishing the quality dimensions of the service, the service organisation can focus on measuring and improving these dimensions. Therefore, dimensions provide a starting point in developing and improving the quality of services.

One of the most widely accepted characteristics of services seems to be heterogeneity. Provided we agree in this respect, from a logical viewpoint we should be very suspicious of rather multidimensional models that are argued to be generalisable to any kind of services or contexts. The heterogeneity of services actually means that their quality dimensions must also be different.

In spite of this, such structural frameworks as the one developed here could be used as checklists for the development of questionnaires. Generally, it is important to take into account the complex relationships of dimensions at the theoretical and empirical levels. In this sense, the framework presented may be a step forward in the continued development of a topology for service quality dimensions.

On the basis of the empirical results, a general conclusion is to be that some quality dimensions used in the models seem to be more important than others. The manifestation and, therefore, usefulness of quality dimensions differ between services.

In this study the three high-level dimensions (physical quality, interactive quality, and corporate quality) matched well to all the case services. The low-level dimensions did not match well to any service and differences were found between the services. In both restaurants almost one-third of the low-level dimensions did not receive any empirical support.

Consequently, the empirical results of this study suggest that there is no self-evident justification to develop or at least generalise multidimensional models for a heterogeneous and abstract area such as service quality. Such models are probably difficult to apply to all service contexts. This means that even for empirical reasons the generalisability of such models as SERVQUAL seems to be limited (cf. Carman, 1990).

To conclude, our study is exploratory and illustrative. However, we believe that there was sufficient evidence to give some important suggestions for the evaluation of quality model development. Regarding future research, the next step might be to repeat the study including additional models and extensive empirical data. Probably, a number of contextual elements should also be taken into account. This kind of research design could lead to new and profound challenges in building service quality models.

References

Armistead, C.G. and C. Wampach, 1988, 'Customer Service in the Context of Food Retailing Operations', in R. Johnston (ed.), *The Management of Service Operations*. London: UK IFS Publications/Springer-Verlag.

Carman, J.M., 1990, 'Consumer Perceptions of Service Quality: An Assessment of the SERVQUAL Dimensions', *Journal of Retailing*, 66, pp. 33-55.

Grönroos, C., 1990, *Service Management and Marketing: Managing the Moments of Truth in Service Competition*. Lexington, Mass.: Lexington Books.

Haywood-Farmer, J., 1990, 'A Conceptual Model of Service Quality', in G. Clark (ed.), *Managing Service Quality*. Kemston: UK IFS Publications, pp.19-25.

Lehtinen, U. and J.R. Lehtinen, 1982, 'Service Quality: A Study of Quality Dimensions', Research Report. Helsinki: Service Management Institute.

Lehtinen, U. and J.R. Lehtinen, 1991, 'Two Approaches to Service Quality Dimensions', *The Service Industries Journal*, (3),pp.289-303.

Parasuraman, A., V.A. Zeithaml and L.L. Berry, 1985, 'A Conceptual Model of Service Quality and Its Implications for Future Research'. *Journal of Marketing* ,49 (Fall), pp.41-50.

Parasuraman, A., V.A. Zeithaml and L.L. Berry, 1988, 'SERVQUAL: A Multiple-Item Scale for Measuring Consumer Perceptions of Service Quality', *Journal of Retailing*, 64, pp.12-40.

Zeithaml, V.A, A. Parasuraman and L.L. Berry, 1990, *Delivering Quality Service: Balancing Customer Perceptions and Expectations*. New York: Free Press.

Subject Index

117

Authors Index